Slinging Ink

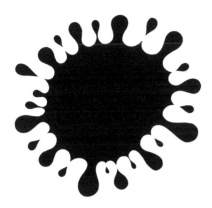

Slinging Ink

A Practical Guide to Producing
Booklets, Newspapers, and Ephemeral Publications

Jan Sutter

William Kaufmann, Inc.
Los Altos, California

Experimental Edition
ISBN 0-86576-037-3
Printed in the United States of America

Library of Congress Cataloging in Publication Data

Sutter, Jan, 1974-
  Slinging ink.

  Bibliography: p.
  1. Printing, Practical—Handbooks, manuals, etc.
I. Title.
Z244.3.S95   686.2'252   82-15179
ISBN 0-86576-037-3   AACR2

"It is a newspaper's duty to print the news and raise hell."

— Wilbur Storey
Chicago Times
1861

**SLINGING
INK**

Contents

I
The Printing Process

II
Writing Copy

III
Interviews

IV
Leaflets and Newsletters

V
Newspapers

VI
Preparation for Layout

VII
Photography and Halftones

VIII
Tools

IX
Typography

X
Staff Organization

XI
Circulation, Advertising and Money Matters

XII
At The Printers

I
The Printing Process

Ever since Johann Gutenberg pieced together the first practical printing device, using the wooden screw from an old wine press in the 15th Century, the world hasn't been the same. His press was a simple affair which lowered a plate or platen against a bed of upraised type, forcing a printed image onto a sheet of paper placed between them. The evolution of printing technology was slow, and it has taken over 500 years to develop Gutenberg's press into its modern counterpart capable of printing up to 25,000 or more impressions per hour. Yet the principle remains the same, and, like Gutenberg's simple invention, the modern press is still a machine designed to hold a printing form or plate in such a way that it can be inked and brought into contact with the paper, transferring the image.

The purpose of this book is to show you how to create leaflets, newsletters and small newspapers in a cheap, efficient and attractive manner. But before jumping into the details of composition and production let's take a brief look at some of the sorts of things you may be interested in producing.

Looking at Some Examples

The following examples include the front page from a community newspaper, various types and styles of leaflets and a sample newsletter. The intent here is to give you some overall idea of what the elements of good makeup are; that is, how the headlines, subheads, text, type style, captions, cartoons, photos and graphics all work together in an organic whole to produce the maximum visual impact.

Newspapers

The GRAPEVINE is an example of a small, photo offset community newspaper. This particular twelve-page issue uses a cartoon to dramatize its lead story. While it is not easy to generalize about make-up, the extent to which a newspaper relies on newsstand sales will influence its front page. Even folded and tossed casually on an office desk or coffee table, a paper should still attract

the eye. Therefore, when the GRAPEVINE is folded horizontally just above the second headline, the cartoon caption remains readable and the front page retains a great deal of its visual impact. This particular issue was produced using an office model IBM Executive typewriter and printed on a large web-type newspress.

Unlike the GRAPEVINE, many small newspapers choose to place no newscopy whatsoever on the front page, relying on the impact of a full page photo or dramatic graphic design to attract the reader. Just what captures the eye best, though, is far from certain. Nonetheless, it seems that if the aspects of content and emotional appeal are the same, a strong but simple poster quality will increase the effectiveness of a front page. From this it follows that a picture with words of the contents will do better than a picture by itself. Worst of all is a cluttered, confused page, where the reader's eye wanders, unable to focus on any distinct image. Our example above shows many aspects of good makeup, including something of a poster quality.

Perhaps at this time it's in order to say a few words about community newspapers and how they differ from their large, city cousins. Many contrasts are obvious. For one thing, community newspapers are

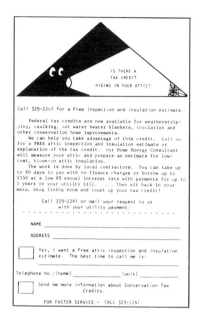

smaller, come out less often and are strongly local in their content. The emphasis is on nearby affairs, particularly politics, and in general they shy away from crime, violence and disaster. Thus they are limited by their nature, and operate on a more personal, close-to-home basis. Yet because they cover a certain geographical area, offer a narrower spectrum of news and respond to different deadlines, they have the opportunity to focus on single issues in an in-depth fashion rarely matched by the large papers.

This goes far in explaining their attraction for the readership. Whereas the daily papers seem distant and impersonal, community papers reflect the lives and times of ordinary people, not just the rich, powerful and famous. People tend to read these papers precisely because they mirror their jobs, organizations, history and lifestyles. By their very nature such papers encourage readers to take an interest and involvement in the goings on of their community by illuminating the inside wheelings and dealings of city hall or the maneuvers over at the school board. Often, small papers contain features and information found nowhere else. These can range from articles on the first settlers of the county to coverage of the local art, music and literary scene to just plain useful suggestions such as where to go and have a good time on Saturday night.

Of course, the GRAPEVINE is only our chosen illustration of a small newspaper. Actually, there are scores of different types of small newspapers other than community newspapers. These range from such familiar examples as the High School News to much more specialized trade and labor publications, each with its own defined audience, special format, selected scope and coverage.

Leaflets and Newsletters

Designing leaflets and newsletters doesn't involve anywhere near the demands of a newspaper. Yet a lot of the same principles of sound makeup used on a newspaper go into them. Study the examples on these pages. Notice how all of them, including the simplest, are graphically inviting. In addition, many have a strong poster quality we discussed before. This poster quality is one aspect that helps them stand out when placed on a wall or bulletin board. In each case, care has been taken in the composition to give the text lots of breathing room, leaving plenty of white space around captions and graphics. White space -- and lots of it -- is one of the secrets of good leaflet design.

Let's look at the leaflets one at a time. Our first example on page 3 is one of the simplest. Attractive and effective, a leaflet like this one can be produced using an IBM Selectric typewriter, a mimeograph and a felt-tipped pen. The humor and charm of the graphic, adding appeal to what otherwise might be a dull subject, is one of its secrets.

Humor, irony and grace contribute to the impact of the other two examples above. Elegantly printed on bond paper, the one on the left can't

help but raise a chuckle -- and cause you to dwell upon its unusual
message. Notice how the author has gone to great lengths in the
makeup, even to the point of indenting the final line to visually balance
the text.

The two remaining examples below are also worth careful study.
The leaflet on the left uses a reversed banner across the top in which
the letters appear in white against an inked background. In addition
to typeset headlines, it employs justified type, where the left and
right text margins are even, as compared to the "ragged" right margin
in the leaflet on page 3. The small, round graphics this example uses
to enhance its appearance and emphasize its theme are miniature works
of art in themselves.

The leaflet on the right does something similar, complementing
its Baroque theme with its graphics and an appearance and choice
of type style similar to that of a theater handbill. Both leaflets, using
an 8 1/2" x 11" format, demonstrate qualities of good makeup, graphic
balance and generous use of white space.

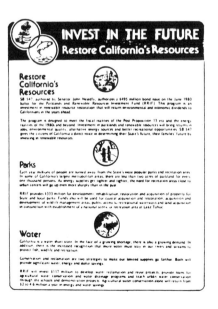

Our last example is a mimeographed newsletter. Notice here, too, the authors pay attention to visual appeal, providing a generous banner on the front page and taking care to give some sort of graphic relief on the inside pages lest the eye get lost in a sea of type. This sort of news-letter is easy to produce as the pages are simply stapled together and the banner, provided with a dateline, can be used over and over again. By varying the color of the paper each issue and changing the front page slightly, the designer makes one issue distinguishable from the next.

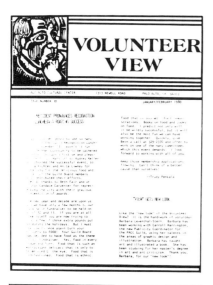

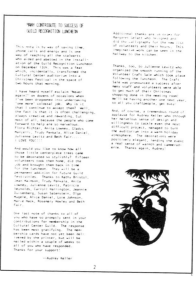

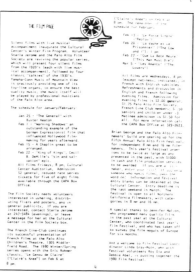

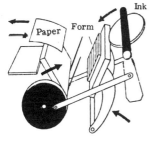

Platen Press

Methods of Reproduction

There are three widely used methods of reproduction to be familiar with. They are the letterpress, photo offset lithography and duplication. Letterpress is the oldest method, but it's slow and costly as compared to photo offset. Duplicators are cheapest. But the results of a mimeograph or ditto lack the beauty and versatility of printed material. Yet they may be quite satisfactory for a leaflet.

Letterpress

This is the earliest adopted process of printing, first used by the Chinese in the 5th Century. It employs a metal of low melting temperature -- often lead -- which allows any quantity of an individual letter or set of letters to be cast in a mold or matrix. Each letter is cast as a raised, backward surface, which when inked will transfer the image to the paper. The paper is fed to the press either by hand or mechanically and ink brought into contact with it by the platen. Letterpress is practical for all types of publications, but it is costly as it often requires the use of a special machine called a linotype to cast the letters into slugs. It works best with high-quality paper because the force of the impression tends to blur on fibrous or rough paper. Letterpress gives the finest quality printing and can print directly from type or the linotype cast slugs.

Lithography

Derived from the process used by artists to produce lithographs, offset lithography is based on the repulsion of ink and water. For example, characters drawn with a grease pencil on the smooth surface of a polished stone will repel water when applied to the surface. The water in turn will repel ink that is rolled across the stone, so when paper is pressed against it, only the image of the drawn character is transferred and printed.

In modern lithography, a photographically engraved zinc plate is usually substituted for the stone and the image is transferred, or offset, onto a rubber blanket which in turn places the image onto the paper. One advantage to offset printing is that its rollers print uniformly on all kinds of paper. Another is that it enables you to print virtually anything that can be photographed. The quality of the product, however, is considered slightly inferior to the letterpress.

Duplicators

Two types of duplicating machines are widely used for preparing leaflets and newsletters. The mimeograph uses a wax-coated stencil, which is typed or drawn upon. The stencil is then wrapped around an ink-filled drum on the mimeo machine. The padded surface of the drum absorbs the ink and forces it through the impressed areas of the stencil, passing the ink to the paper. Mimeograph uses a somewhat coarse-grained paper which is inexpensive.

The other kind of duplicator, universally known as a ditto machine, also uses a master sheet to produce the image. This master is a carbon-coated sheet which is written, typed or drawn upon. The dye from the sheet is pressure transferred to the master which is then placed upon the drum of the ditto machine. An alcohol-based fluid dissolves the thin layer of dye from the master, which is then brought in contact with the paper.

Worknotes

A Few Useful Terms

Provided on the following pages are a few useful terms and their definitions. It's a good idea to read them over a couple of times to become familiar with them. Even a modest working knowledge of the language of the printshop can save you time, money and heart-break. The list is nowhere near conclusive, but it will help you become used to the jargon of printing.

Halftone Process: Used to reproduce photographs in the printed media. Halftoning is the photomechanical system by which continuous tones are photographed through a special ruled halftone screen. This process converts the tones into tiny dot formations which, when printed, optically render the tonal graduations of the original photograph. Both the printing plate and the impression made from it are called halftones.

Leaflet: A single printed sheet, sometimes folded once or twice.

Folder: A printed sheet folded several times.

Broadside: A large folder.

Envelope stuffer: A single sheet, printed on one side, generally featuring a specific product or service and often included with a monthly billing or periodic mailing. The examples on page 5 are envelope stuffers.

Handbill: A single printed sheet usually distributed from door to door. Handbills are sometimes called "throwaways," as that is often their fate once they reach the hands of the recipient.

Engraving: A general term for any relief printing plate produced by hand, photomechanically or electrically.

Etching: Biting an image into a metal plate by either chemical or electrolytic process.

Offset printing: A printing process in which an image is offset on an intermediate cylinder before being transferred to the paper. In modern usage, offset, photo offset and photo lithography are interchangable terms. There is no practical distinction between them.

Photoengraving: An etched relief printing plate produced for the letterpress process by means of photography. The process involves exposing film negatives to sensitized metal, causing the image to become acid resistant. The nonprinting areas are then etched with acid to the required relief.

Positive: A transparent or printed image where the light and dark areas correspond to those of the original subject.

Negative: A transparent or printed image where the light and dark areas are reversed from the original subject.

Makeup: The process of hand arranging the lines of type, headlines, subheads, captions and text in the position in which they will appear in the printed piece as specified by the layout.

Stripping: The process of assembling in negative form all the elements which are to appear on the printing plate. Many times illustrations, graphics or photographs are supplied separately from the rest of the material to be put together. These graphics may be larger or smaller than they are to appear in the finished product. They are photographically blown up or down to the proper size and "stripped" into position on the master negative or flat.

Opaquing: Applying red or black pigment to photographic negatives in order to block the passage of light and get rid of undesirable mistakes or blemishes on the negative. This operation is usually performed by hand, using a brush.

II
Writing Copy

The Five W's and the H Formula

> The admission that the Titanic, the biggest
> steam ship in the world, had been sunk by an
> iceberg and had gone to the bottom of the Atlan-
> tic, probably carrying more than 1,400 of her
> passengers, was made at the White Star Line
> offices, 9 Broadway at 8:20 o'clock last night.
>
> Then, P.A.S. Franklin, Vice President and
> General Manager of the International Merchan-
> tile Marine, conceded that probably only those
> passengers who were picked up by the Cunarder
> Carpathia had been saved. Advices received
> early this morning tend to increase the number
> of survivors by 200 ...

Thus a reporter for the New York Times composed the opening
front page lead on April 16, 1912, for what was to be one of the worst
ocean disasters of all time.

It's worthwhile to take a few moments and examine the traditional
approach to composing news copy, for there is much to be learned
from this type of writing. To begin, observe how much information
is packed into the above two paragraphs. Next, notice that even
though the story is almost three-quarters of a century old, it still
reads much like what you might expect to see in a newspaper today.
This is because it makes use of a number of proven devices found in
good news copy writing, among them the construction of a lead paragraph containing the what, where, when, who, why and how of the
story, the so-called five w's and the h.

The use of the five w's and the h, in conjunction with a lead paragraph summing up the essence of the story, has been pounded into the heads of aspiring young reporters for generations. Sometimes a half dozen short one-sentence paragraphs are used. Yet seldom does the lead exceed more than 75 words. Regardless, the idea is to sum up as briefly as possible the story as a whole. Then, in the following copy, it can be retold and embellished in a spiraling pattern of diminishing importance.

Be aware that this is mechanically different from any other written forms you may have mastered or suffered under -- the essay, poetry, novel, short story, stage drama, or English 1B composition. The reason for this is that news writers turn fiction conventions on their heads. Here the climax comes first. Unlike a dime store thriller, the "who done it" is at the beginning and the rest of the clues come later. Even for those who don't intend to write news copy, it's a technique worth mastering, because it's an effective and logical way of composing copy. In terms of the Times story, the formula is as follows:

What?	The admission that the Titanic has been sunk
Where?	at the bottom of the Atlantic
Who?	P.A.S. Franklin, Vice President
When?	8:20 o'clock last night
Why/how?	by an iceberg

The details of the why and how make up the rest of the story, the portion that's called the body. In traditional news reporting the body is organized in a deliberate fashion known as an inverted pyramid. That is, the most important facts come first and the copy tapers off to less important items.

With this in mind, let's take another look at the structure of a news story. Our example this time comes from the Times's competitor of the day, the New York Herald. Contrast this paper's florid style with that of the rather staid Times. Note, however, that the technique of composition is much the same. Again, the lead paragraph both introduces the story and sums up the essence of the copy, the sinking of the <u>Titanic</u>.   See how many of the five <u>w</u>'s and the <u>h</u> you can pick out in its forty-word lead paragraph.

> The Titanic Sinks With 1800 Persons Onboard
>
> Most appalling disaster in marine history occurs when world's largest steamship strikes gigantic iceberg at night --
>
> In the darkness of night and in water two miles deep the <u>Titanic</u>, newest of the White Star Fleet and greatest of all ocean steamships, sank to the bottom of the sea twenty minutes past two o'clock yesterday morning.
>
> Dispatches received late last night from the Cape Race wireless station in Newfoundland and admissions reluctantly made at the same time by the New York officials of the White Star Company warrant the fear that of the 2,200 persons who were aboard the great vessel when she received her mortal wound in the collision with an iceberg more than 1,500 have gone to their deaths in her shattered hulk, while 675, most of whom are women and children, have been saved.
>
> Should these grim figures be verified, the loss of the <u>Titanic</u> -- costliest, most powerful, greatest of all the ocean fleet -- while speeding westward on her maiden voyage will take rank in maritime history as the most terrible of all recorded disasters of the sea.
>
> There is yet, no information as to those who are among the saved and the greater number of the unfortunates who must be numbered with the lost. The officers of the White Star Company themselves at the hour of going to press had been unable to learn the details of the horror that will carry grief into a thousand American homes, some of them among the proudest in the metropolis ...

NEWS STRUCTURE

Lead &
Main facts

Lesser

Trivia

This story is a good example of inverted pyramid structuring, where the most important aspects are given in the lead, and the copy progresses downward in order of diminishing importance. Upon closer examination it becomes apparent that the technique offers a number of advantages when it comes to composing copy. For one thing, it channels interest immediately into the body of copy, the lead paragraph acting as a sort of funnel through which the reader is introduced promptly to the subject. In addition, the lead summary structure lets readers know quickly if they are interested in reading further. Finally, because the copy is composed in this fashion, it's possible to skim only the first half of a story, yet learn the essentials.

In news work, there are also a couple of distinct reasons for favoring this form which facilitates layout in general and makes life easier for the press crew. This is because copy readers automatically know that the least important items are last. Therefore, at paste-up time, if a story needs to be cut to fit the space available, it gets chopped from the bottom. Last, but not least important, inverted pyramid structuring also aids the person making headlines. If a story is composed in this fashion, the headline maker need only glance at the first two or three paragraphs to get an idea of what the copy contains.

Incidentally, it's said that the inverted pyramid structure was invented by an enterprising young reporter during the Civil War when news was transmitted from the battlefield by telegraph to the Northern presses. It was reasoned at the time that if the lines were cut in the thick of the fight or sabotaged by marauding bands, the most important items of news were more likely to reach their destination.

Thus, when a transmission was interrupted, the anxious editors
at the other end automatically understood that anything that might
have followed was of lesser importance.

What's a News Story?

So what's a news story? Basically it's a factual report of what
happened. In bare bones, it tries to tell the readers what happened,
why and how in the briefest, clearest and most accurate manner
possible.

The why and how, however, are often the monkey wrench. To
many journalists, these are more than likely the essence of the news
story. To say that a man was imprisoned for theft is one thing. But
to say that he stole a loaf of bread to feed his starving family and was
caught in the act may be something else entirely.

Thus crops up the specter of interpretation. That is, which facts
does a reporter play up? Which are indeed important and which secondary?   Seldom do responsible newspeople pander to an audience. But
to those interested in the social forces behind events, the ideal posture
might well be something other than the vaunted "impartiality" or strict
"objectivity." Or to put it in other terms, are there always two sides
to every issue? Can there be only a single interpretation of an event?
Or can there be sixteen?

Patterns of News Story Structure

Let's turn once again to basic news story structure. Nearly 90%
of all news stories conform to definite patterns. Below we'll examine
the fundamental block structure of three standard types of reporting.
They are the fact, action and quote variations.

Our first example is a factual story. Here the thing to pay
attention to is the tapering structure in which the most important, eye-
catching facts come first, followed by those of less significance.

SENIOR PROGRAM AXED

Lead -- contains who,
what, when, etc.

The Grey Ghost, a controversial rehabilitation project nationally noted for its success in dealing with the problems of aging and retirement, lost its funding June 2, marking the end of a long running battle with the city council.   The Ghost's active attempts to influence and initiate various legislative measures was cited by various council members as the reason for the fund cut.   The final vote was eight to two to discontinue the program.

Second fact --

Axing of the project came as no surprise to those who followed the recent city elections.   This May, in campaigns wracked with distortions, misrepresentations and at times downright lies from both sides, pro-business candidates Witherspoon, Clay and Evans mounted a blistering single-issue campaign against the Ghost and similar socially oriented programs.

Third fact --

Many believe the Ghost was sacked because of its unusual approach to the problems of senior citizens. Members of the project maintained the the majority of problems faced by the older community could not be resolved until what they termed the 'underlying myths' that older people are no longer productive members of society are dispelled.   To this end, the group engaged in actively supporting measures aimed at abolishing mandatory retirement at age 65.

Fourth fact --

Few questioned the overall success of the program.   Social workers from the office of Health, Education and Welfare say there is a direct relationship between the program's approach and its effectiveness.

Less important facts --	Other experts pointed to a year-long evaluation of the project by the Robert F. Kennedy Institute for Aging which gave it a favorable review.
Less important facts --	At the council meeting, thirty-six members of the community argued to save the program. A petition with over 2,000 signatures supporting the project was presented. However a majority of the council remained unconvinced.
Least important facts --	Most council members took part in the debate. Chairwoman Enid Ray, in the minority, praised the Grey Ghost. "This is an effective program," she said, "We must fund it."
Least important facts --	Two conservative members of the council, however, Clay and Walters, seemed to have already made up their minds. Early in the evening they absented themselves from the hearings.
Trivia --	Later, the two admitted that they had ducked out for a pizza at the Round Table while the community members addressed the remaining council.

The Fact Story

Regardless of how a story is written, it's important to remember that most stories lose nearly half their readers after the headline and first paragraph. Still more readers drop off after the second or third. But if a story is structured in a tapering fashion, a person in a hurry can read only the first paragraph and get a good idea of what's going on.

One reason readers can be lost is the way a story looks. If it appears hard to read, they may choose to go no farther. Visual appeal has to do not only with layout but also with how the writer arranges the paragraphs. In the example, the tendency is to alternate short- and medium-length paragraphs. Notice, in addition, that the last three paragraphs could be cut entirely without destroying the story. For that matter, tight for space, the copy crew might paste up only the first three paragraphs and still get the message across.

The Action Story

Let's look at another type of story, the action story. Action stories read something like eyewitness accounts. There is a "we were there" quality about them. Often they are written in the present tense and in general they are more difficult to write than fact stories. One problem is that in arranging a narrative action, the reporter must juggle dramatic incidents, description, setting and testimony, as well as explanatory data, in a cohesive fashion. Meanwhile, the story tries to adhere to the pyramid structure format.

Notice how our action story below interlocks in a chronological manner. Things take on the illusion that they are physically happening. The reader enters the tense council room, where the police stand in the aisles as angered community members confront bureaucrats. The action cuts to the pacing project director, then on to the wounded WWI veteran's impassioned plea. It moves to the taut roll call vote and finally ends with a vindictive council member bawling into the microphone as mad citizens file out the door of city hall.

How is all this accomplished? The secret is a tell, retell, and retell again method. That is, the whole story is told briefly in the lead. Then, it's told in detail again, and retold more fully in following paragraphs. In the end, the reader arrives at the fine details, but all in the told, retold, and retold-in-more-detail format.

The real beauty of this style of writing, however, is its dramatic quality. The action style of narration is especially powerful because the reader is encouraged to "see" the news unfolding before his eyes.

COUNCIL DUMPS SENIOR PROGRAM

Lead, told in an
at-the-scene style --

With uniformed city police monitoring an overflow crowd of hundreds, thirty-six members of the community addressed the city council in a last ditch effort to save the Grey Ghost, a controversial program for senior citizens.

More at-the-scene
details and facts --

But with the clock pushing midnight and the final eight-to-two vote cast, the Ghost -- which had the support of thousands of members of the community, including social workers, psychiatrists, psychologists, state and county health people, teachers, students and older persons in general -- was stripped of operating funds.

More detail --

Angrily pacing the chamber carpet, Ginny Redgrave, the project's director, explained how the group viewed its work. She emphasized that within our country there exist particular attitudes which lead to neglect of the elderly and contribute to unemployment, job frustration, poor housing, bad health care, illness and poverty among the aging.

Facts --

In the absence of hope for change, she argued, people turn to despair. A lot of the so-called health problems of older citizens, she maintained, are a direct result of society's denial of an older person's self worth.

At-the-scene detail --

His throat choked with emotion, a decorated WWI veteran told of his own personal frustrations with the Veterans Administration and his ever-dwindling Social Security check. William Norton, 82, partially disabled and leaning on a cane, spoke of his difficulty in securing proper medical attention for wounds he received half a century ago at Verdun.

Facts --

He stated that the Grey Ghost was one community group not only willing to aid him in securing a necessary operation, but in addition, the project found him suitable part time employment, enabling him to live independently. "Whether it was standing by the telephone in the middle of the night, or arranging an emergency ride to the hospital -- this is one program that really cares," he told the audience.

At-the-scene --

In the end, however, the council remained unconvinced. As the clerk intoned a roll call vote to cut off funds, it was evident few had been swayed.

Facts and details --

Conservative councilman Freeman Evans seemed especially vindictive toward those fighting for funding. As the audience filed from the chambers, he bawled into the microphone:

Detail --

"Next time maybe you socially concerned types will be more conciliatory. Now maybe you'll learn not to dabble in politics without approval of the council."

The Quote Story

Let's turn to a third variation of the basic news story structure. This is the quote format. It's done as a follow-up to the previous coverage of the city council meeting.

Speeches, statements, eyewitness accounts, interviews -- all often fall in the category of quote stories. They are based on oral or written information, transcribed by reporters or taken from tapes, court records or other sources. Like the action story, the quote story may also convey a dramatic or at-the-scene quality.

One of the simplest structures of a quote story is the summary-quote, summary-quote arrangement. The example is arranged with a lead summary, a "link" paragraph connecting the lead to the body and then an alternating summary-quote, summary-quote story. Again, the diminishing importance, inverted pyramid style is maintained. Another thing to note here, also, is that the physical size of the paragraphs has a tendency to visually enforce the inverted pyramid effect.

This is a very simple method of construction, but it is also a very powerful one. Faced with the task of sorting through thousands of words and summarizing them in a meaningful way, a reporter tries to select the most eye-catching, meaningful or pertinent statements and arrange them into a condensed story which hangs together well. In addition to direct quote and summary structure, other devices are often employed in quote stories, including the use of indirect quotes, as in the example below, together with general serial condensation.

SENIORS FIGHT BACK

Lead --

Angered by yesterday's city council move to deny funding to the Grey Ghost, a controversial senior citizen's group, Ginny Redgrave, the program's director, spoke to an assembled group of over 300 at noon today on the steps of city hall.

Link --

Ms. Redgrave and others backing the Grey Ghost's unique program have decided to take the issue directly to the voters in the form of a referendum. Addressing a crowd of supporters, she explained why the city should be forced into continuing to fund the project.

Quote --

"Last Friday I was in the emergency room at county hospital when an elderly man was wheeled in dead. His phone had been cut off the week previous after his social security check had failed to come. Neighbors found him unconscious in the bathroom, unable to summon help. He had been there two days."

Indirect quote --

Redgrave then went on to explain how neglect of the elderly is not just an individual problem, but in fact is the result of a social process. To isolate the individual cases, she said, and not the attitude which encourages the problem, is no solution.

Quote --

"The doctor at the hospital didn't have to ponder why the man was dead. Already he knew about the cut-off phone and I overheard him tell one of the nurses, "This death was needless, an hour, two hours earlier, we could have saved him."

Summary --

Meanwhile, as Redgrave spoke, a community-wide coalition was being formed in support of the Ghost. Besides gathering signatures for a referendum, the group is sponsoring a recall election to unseat certain city council members.

Quote --

"It's time we dragged some of the city council into the 20th Century," said decorated WWI veteran William Norton, a Grey Ghost supporter.

Summary --

The crowd voiced its approval as ten coalition members fanned through the audience with clipboards and petitions.

Quote --

"Who says you can't fight city hall!" came a shout from the crowd as a curious public began to join the ensemble.

Leads

It's an old newspaper saying that "with the lead written -- the story's half done." In fiction the opening scene is a hook upon which the reader hangs the imagination. So too with a news lead. That is, it's the lead's function to act as a hook to attract the reader's attention. But more than that, it's a springboard from which to launch the whole story. Since originality and visual impression are the essence of a good lead, leads tend to be as diverse as the people who create them. Yet there are a few ground rules. For example, many of the five w's and the h are routinely contained in the various types of leads. Below are a few of these variations.

Cartridge lead --   The war in Xanadu is over.
                     President O'Hara resigned today.
                     Mayor Bradley died in office this morning.

The cartridge lead is generally used on occasions of historical importance, but it can be used successfully on more local issues. It gets its name because, like a cartridge or bullet, it goes straight to the mark.

Punch lead --   Three members of the Metropolis police Special Readiness Team were arraigned today in federal court on charges of gun running.

The punch lead is very similar to the cartridge, but generally it's a little longer. The effect is the same, though. It's written for pow or punch -- a direct bull's-eye hit. Some examples include:

Summary lead --   Thirty-five riders on a Western Pacific commuter train narrowly escaped injury when a runaway locomotive rammed into their coach this morning.

Visual lead --   Hurling quarts of day-glo paint as riot
                                 clad officers closed in, dozens of angry
                                 street artists and poets made a valiant,
                                 if desperate, last ditch stand against a
                                 local ordinance prohibiting sidewalk
                                 vending.

Question lead --   Have you registered to vote? No? Then
                                 you'd better do it by tomorrow if you
                                 want a say in the controversial Willow
                                 Road development.

Tie-back lead --   Ignoring a third federal restraining order
                                 against mass picketing, striking workers
                                 at Tri-Con, a local electronics firm, once
                                 again succeeded in shutting down the plant.

Quotation lead --   "We're going to put this crooked commis-
                                 sion out of business," exclaimed local In-
                                 dependent Party leader Michael Fox before
                                 a packed audience during last night's tu-
                                 multuous housing meeting.

The five w's and the h can also be used as leads themselves, as mentioned
before. Here are three examples below:

When --   Wrapping up a two-hour investigation this
                                 morning, police revealed that clever bur-
                                 glars, tunneling their way into Bimbo's
                                 Burger Bliss on Main, had gotten away.

Who --   A team of skillful burglars, burrowing
                                 their way into Bimbo's Burger Bliss last
                                 night, absconded with more than $2,500
                                 from a locked strongbox.

How --   Under the cover of heavy rains, using
                                 meticulous timing, alpine axes and pow-
                                 erful flashlights, a team of thieves suc-
                                 cessfully tunneled into Bimbo's Burger
                                 Bliss last night.

The variations of a good lead are virtually infinite.   An adept writer can usually evolve a lead by mental process of elimination. The experienced reporter may do it seemingly all at once, but in reality, she or he has written it over numerous times mentally before tackling the typewriter.   In the following example, we'll try to capture some of that process on paper.

Evolution of a lead

Facts --	Citizens are mad ... over the possibility of a nuclear theft or contamination ... they have asked a federal judge to take action ... they filed a federal suit against the Metropolis Research Institute ... The issue? The possible theft of plutonium from the MRI labs.
Rough --	Concerned about the possibilities of nuclear theft, citizens asked for a federal restraining order to stop Metropolis Research Institute from using plutonium in its research.
Finished --	"The possibility of plutonium theft to manufacture a crude bomb is real," charged a citizens' affidavit filed today before federal judge Connie Wilson in an attempt to halt atomic experiments at Metropolis Research Institute.

Brevity and Clarity

A few things still remain to be pointed out.   One is the importance of brevity.   Nothing can kill even the best story faster than a crowded and vague lead.   Brevity and clarity are essential to any type of news reporting.   So are conciseness and the use of uncluttered and buttressing detail.

Another thing that can greatly improve your writing style is use of the active voice.   One valid criticism of our New York Times copy on page 11 is that it is written in a passive voice.   Today's editors stressing the use of active verbs, might change the lead to read something like this: "The admission that the <u>Titanic</u>, biggest steamship in the world, was sunk by an iceberg, going to the bottom of the Atlantic with more than 1,400 of her passengers ...."

Once in a while there are instances where a writer faces an assignment impossible to summarize in a single lead. In this case, two or three paragraphs may be called for. Confronted with a story this complicated, it may well prove easier to write two or more stories spotlighting different aspects of the same events. This is especially true of stories dealing with confrontation or those having "two sides." Thus, even though it's important to strive for brevity, don't feel compelled to cram everything into a single column. In many cases, sidelights, spot items, interviews or features connected with the main item enhance the issue. This is especially true if written by different authors.

Composing Copy for Leaflets and Newsletters

What about composing copy for leaflets and newsletters? Well, fortunately, here too, the same general rules apply as in news work. For example, it's almost always best to introduce your topic immediately with a lead sentence or paragraph that gets straight to the point. A good idea is to aim at both introducing and summing up the essence of your message in about 75 words or less. Remember, it's very likely half of the readers will only casually skim the first paragraph or two, so it's important to get as much as you can across there.

Next, arrange the copy so that the most important items appear first and the ones of lesser value follow in an order of diminishing importance. Remember to back up any arguments you make with buttressing details and concrete examples. When composing copy be careful not to make the paragraphs so long and ponderous as to frighten the reader off. Best, if possible, is to alternate short- and medium-length paragraphs whenever possible. Enliven your style when writing by using the active rather than passive voice, and above all, strive to be brief, clear and to the point.

Worknotes

Where do most news stories come from? How do you go about getting a story? Then how do you write it? The secret of writing a good article is knowing what you want to say and then saying it clearly. If you don't know what you are talking about, chances are your readers won't either.

Most stories are arrived at through a combination of direct interviews and research. It's hard to overstress the value of direct contact with a source. A few direct quotes from someone intimately involved in a story can often carry more authenticity than two dozen paragraphs tediously compiled in a library. On the other hand, research is invaluable in conducting a good interview. Good research enables you to ask the right questions. Hard facts interwoven with direct quotes can result in dynamite copy.

Another thing is not to be overly shy about taking sides, making judgments or being partisan. But be straight with the reader. If you do make a judgment about something, support what you say with fact and logic.

In the end, good advice is to write like you speak. Beware of sounding like a Philadelphia lawyer. Stay away from fancy words and complicated sentence structure. If you think a word is unfamiliar to readers, define it in the text. Better yet, find a simpler one. Long sentences can almost always be cut into two or more short ones.   Once you have finished a first draft, go back and simplify sentences and paragraphs. Two or three short paragraphs invite reading a lot more than will a single, long monster.

Hints on Researching Articles

Most information you need is not secret. Usually it is published somewhere in newspapers, books, reports or other documents and records. One of the best places to start when researching a local story is with the established commercial newspapers.

Commercial Press

Keeping up with the larger commercial papers is an essential part of a community newspaper's routine. Surveying the general news pages will keep you up on the local issues, people in the news and important upcoming meetings and events. Pay particularly close attention to state and local political news and keep a clipping file for reference. The society, business and legal sections can also be valuable sources of information. Keep in mind that all newspapers have their own clipping files or morgues, as they are sometimes called. If you can gain access to these, they are invaluable sources of background, historical and local information. Try buttonholing a sympathetic reporter, or adopt the cover of a student doing thesis research.

Libraries

Don't overlook the city library. This can be a gold mine of information. Not only will it have back issues of the local commercial press, but very often there may also be chronological indexes of subjects and topics. If you are fortunate, a historical librarian may be able to turn you on to special collections of pictures, books and newspapers about your community. Another person to seek out is the reference librarian. He or she can be very helpful in locating and steering you to the information you have been looking for.

If the library has a special section or branch devoted to business periodicals, reference work or other literature, check it out. Don't overlook the publications of the local Chamber of Commerce, the JAYCEES or other business organizations. These sources can pro-

vide excellent insight on proposed commercial development and the
plans for the community.

Government Agencies

Government agencies are another indispensable source of information. Many state and federal agencies are required by law to have public documents open for inspection. But "Right to Know" or "Freedom
of Information" laws are often vague and confusing. So if you expect
problems getting what you need, have a friendly lawyer or law student
check out the situation beforehand. Such laws usually cover access
to administrative regulations, studies, reports, names and salaries
of government officials, correspondence, minutes of meetings and
things considered to be public records. But just because you may
have a legal right to information doesn't mean you're going to have
an easy time getting it. If government officials refuse to release
data, you can:

-- Have a sympathetic lawyer give them a call and suggest to them
   that they comply with the law. If they resist, you can threaten
   legal action.
-- Ask to speak to their superiors. Often times, low-level government employees are reluctant to comply with unusual requests
   without an okay from above.
-- As a last resort there is always the option of finding someone
   inside the agency with a key to the photocopier and the willingness
   to provide what you wish to know.

For federal documents not immediately available, try your con-
gressperson or senator first or write directly to the federal agency
or congressional committee involved before sending off to the U.S.
Government Printing Office. This can save time and money, as usually you'll get the documents faster and free of charge.

Universities

Large colleges and universities have not only good libraries but also reports, dissertations, references and pamphlets about your community, region and state. Most social science departments have a couple of professors or graduate students who have researched local issues. They can provide overview and background information as well as specific leads.

How to Find Out Who Somebody Is

Let's say that you know the name of a city council member, local slum lord, welfare commissioner or corporate executive, but nothing more. How do you find out who this person really is? The information you want usually includes address, business and family connections, real estate holdings, and life-style -- including church, school and social connections as well as the person's influence in the local power structure. You can undoubtedly obtain a good deal of information by talking with informal sources, but don't overlook such things as public directories, records and other written documents. Sources include:

The Telephone Book

Great for addresses and phone numbers.   You can find out where the local slum lord lives as well as the location of local agencies, unions, community organizations and the like.

Polk's City Directory

This includes names, addresses, phone numbers, occupations and places of employment of many families, businesses and organizations in the city.

Newspaper Clippings

You can obtain these from the local library, or other sources, such as individuals interested in specific issues.

Court and Tax Records

For these, try the county clerk's office. Court records are filed in the office by docket number. The case record includes the charge, previous record, name of attorney, verdict and sentence. Cross reference by name is provided so you can get the docket number. Tax records give the property owner's name, assessed values, lot location and similar information.

Who's Who

Take a look at Who's Who in America, Who's Who in Commerce and Industry or other sources like Current Biography Yearbook.

Poor's Register of Directors

This is great for listing important corporate directors in the United States. A good tool for researching local corporate power structure.

Moody's Banks

Lists directors of local banks and background on financial dealings. Other corporate information can be found in Moody's or Poor's industrial directories.

League of Women Voters

These folks often provide the best know-your-city booklets describing state and local governments and their functions. They also have information and analyses of various legislative issues.

Committee on Political Education (COPE)

This is the AFL-CIO's political arm. COPE often provides good analysis of political issues which affect organized labor. It also compiles voting records and economic statistics of interest to working people.

Good Government Groups

Civic leagues and the like are often good sources for the dirt in local government and politics.

Chamber of Commerce

Check out its library and files.

People

All of the above should lead you to individuals. Professionals enjoy giving out information. Many people have an ax to grind. Personal contact while doing research is very important for leads and information. Listen to what people have to say. Ask questions. Follow that story!

III
Interviews

It often happens that the best sources of information are direct eyewitness accounts or interviews of principal participants in an event. Face-to-face conversation, information-seeking phone calls, eyewitness reports: all fall into the category of interviews. Inevitably, when gathering information, a reporter may consult a number of individuals before writing anything. Yet, even when the final copy never mentions the original source, it doesn't necessarily mean a lot of people weren't talked to. Indeed, if it weren't for interviews there would be precious little fresh information contained in any newspaper -- community or otherwise.

Therefore, interviews are conducted for a number of reasons. One reason is to gather information. Another is to solicit opinions. A third is to capture a sense of personality for use in a feature story.

When discussing interviews, it's hard to overstress the importance of being prepared. This means knowing exactly what information you're interested in, what questions to ask and how to ask them. Community journalists, especially those interested in social issues, may face special problems when seeking information from public officials and authorities. This can be particularly true if the source has reason to believe the information might wind up putting them in a critical light. "Getting in trouble with my boss," a common and well-founded fear, may make people employed in public positions reluctant to talk to the community press.

Getting the Facts

Frankness and fairness are always good guidelines when dealing with individuals. So as a rule, the best posture for anyone searching for the facts is a straightforward, direct approach. This is all the more true when soliciting an interview. Here a writer does well to identify himself immediately. This is a good idea, even if you have a philosophical disagreement or personal dislike for the individual.

Self assurance on the part of the interviewer is another aspect -- somewhat in the realm of psychological gamesmanship -- which should be understood. It's wise to be neither humble nor arrogant when asking questions. Sometimes it's helpful to put up the appearance that you know as much or more about the topic than the person being interviewed, even though this may all be bluff. After all, "the public has a right to know."

In the end, you may find yourself a cross between a crusading muckraker, detective, confidential friend, psychiatrist and agressive district attorney. But beware, the potential for ego inflation and its accompanying pitfalls is virtually limitless.

Planning an Interview

All interviews contain common elements, but it's the reporter's job to determine the purpose of the interview and go from there. There is no single style, approach or technique that will give good results in every situation, but as mentioned before, preparation and focus cannot be overemphasized.   If an interview is to be successful, the journalist must know beforehand the central focus of the subject to be covered and the boundaries of less important areas.   That is, you must know what you're going to talk about and what you're not.

Therefore, it becomes important to decide prior to the interview what types of information are relevant to the subject you are investigating. Once you decide this, the next job is to formulate the questions which will get the best response. One aid is an interview guide, which can consist of an outline of the topic, a sequence of questions and a checklist of things to cover. Such an outline can also serve as a recording sheet for answers.

Once the questions are formulated, it's necessary to decide what overall strategy, tactics and techniques to use to obtain the answers you desire. Will the interview be scheduled or unscheduled? Unscheduled interviews are good for discovery, but generally, a scheduled interview with tight topic control will result in more complete, in-depth information. In addition, if the person being questioned has a clear understanding of the purpose of the interview, he or she is more likely to provide specific answers.

So if an interview is to be successful, the journalist must know from the start what to ask and why to ask it. Next, it is necessary to clearly communicate these specific questions to the person being interviewed and be able to detect and correct any misunderstandings. Finally, while asking questions and recording answers, the person doing the interview must be careful to guide the person questioned in order to avoid anything irrelevant. Let's take the political interview as an example.

The Political Interview

Lois Lane wants to interview gubernatorial hopeful George McMurphy. She intends to do it in an in-depth, critical fashion. So her first task is to research Mr. McMurphy's legislative record thoroughly. Turning over old news clippings, she comes across the fact that while a state senator, the multimillionaire paid no income taxes. She discovers similar contradictions in McMurphy's

political and personal past. Next, Ms. Lane phones the local labor
council to get its view. She also calls the opposition parties.
Later, our reporter seeks out biographical material in the local
library. Lois doesn't overlook the reference librarian who directs
her to the Los Angeles Times and New York Times indexes. The
reference desk also keeps its own file on political figures. Somehow,
along the way, Lois finds the time to bone up on McMurphy's previous
movie career.

Back in the office, she telephones as many of the opposition
candidates as possible to get more information. She talks with
other reporters on the staff. In the end, she asks McMurphy headquarters to send over a packet on their candidate. Lois reads everything thoroughly. Then she checks and cross-checks, reviewing the
information for accuracy.

Well aware that Mr. McMurphy has spent a lifetime in the public
limelight, Lois knows that the candidate is tuned in to all the public
relations tricks. She understands that he may be counting on intimi-
dating her with his authority and slick image.   So having prepared
as carefully as possible, she begins to outline the questions she wants
to ask. Lois knows what McMurphy's likely response to some of her
questions will be, therefore she prepares follow-up questions to try
to pin the candidate down to specifics.

Having completed these preparations, our reporter decides her
best angle is to try and get the jump on the candidate, train her guns
as squarely as possible and hammer away with tough, to-the-point
questions. She opts to open with the "why no income tax" question and persist from there. She already anticipates McMurphy's
best answer and is ready to interrupt or interject another telling question if he evades the issue or talks off the point.

A veteran reporter, Ms. Lane understands this is not an easy assignment. For this reason she prepares factually and psychologically.
She's no-nonsense about her job and realizes that the best questions

are not easy or obvious ones.   Her strategy is to ask unanticipated
yet highly relevant questions, backed by thorough investigation.

The Approach

Whether you're interviewing a big-time politician or a sub-clerk
in the murky back offices of the city hall, the smart approach is
still the direct one.   The best start is simply to say you are from
X newspaper or organization and that you need information on Y.
Ninety percent of the time you will get the information needed.
Being friendly and natural is almost always helpful, too.   Always
keep in mind that although your paper may be the smallest press
in town, it's a respectable and legitimate publication and doesn't
beg for favors.

Getting Down to Talk

Common sense and being able to think on your feet count heavily
when it comes down to the actual interview.   Dialogue that begins
naturally and proceeds in a friendly and informal way almost always
gets the best results.   A hard-boiled approach or turning on the heat
is an extreme to be resorted to only on rare occasions.

Begin with an introduction and handshake.   The initial dialogue
may be light, friendly and bear on matters of small consequence.
But a successful interview gets down to business quickly, with the
dialogue rapidly channeled into the areas of chartered discussion.
When things warm up, and the journalist is lucky, dialogue begins
to die away and monologue takes over -- the monologue of the person being interviewed.

Keeping the attention of the person being interviewed is most
important.   Eye contact is a must.   The interviewer should listen
as if he or she were vitally interested in every word, as nothing
dampens an interview more quickly than the appearance of bore-
dom.   One final thing to remember is to try to keep things on an

even keel, even if what you're being told has tremendous news value.
If you express excitement, the subject may hedge or qualify.

Obstacles in an Interview

Time conflicts: A busy person may be reluctant to be interviewed
because of a tight time schedule. One way to obtain cooperation is
by selling the idea of the importance of the interview and stressing
the value of the information. Another way of avoiding the problem
of conflicting time demands is to schedule the interview at a time
when there is less competition for a person's attention.   Thus you
might have second thoughts about the wisdom of interviewing can-
nery workers concerning job conditions Friday afternoon following
work, or questioning working mothers at supper time.

Threats to self image: People can withhold information just because
they feel that the interviewer will disapprove or that public disclosure
may embarrass them. A person may well be in a position to lose status or get into trouble with superiors if information becomes public.
In this case, an assurance that the replies will remain anonymous is
important. Made to feel that they will not be endangered or embar-
rassed, respondents are more likely to divulge relevant information.
Another twist to this inhibition arises when people are reluctant to
give candid responses simply out of etiquette or when they think answer-
ing in an honest fashion would be poor taste.

Unpleasant experiences: People can hold back information simply
because of unpleasant feelings associated with an experience. Questions about the death of a loved one, a serious injury on the job, or an
ugly divorce may force a person to relive something which is extremely
uncomfortable. Any of these common occurrences can be painful and
reduce a person's willingness to talk. A little sensitivity and empathy,
plus the ability to put yourself in another's shoes, goes a long way
when faced with this type of situation.

Positive Forces in an Interview

"I'm not much of a talker," said Wayne, cutting the engine and climbing off his forklift. "Don't know much about this here situation with the Teamsters, either. But jawing with you sounds a lot more fun than shuffling boxes in the warehouse."

In this instance, a seasoned interviewer would have recognized immediately one of the common facilitators of an interview -- the simple need expressed by the forklift operator for new experience, a break in the routine, a desire to talk over coffee. Taking advantage of these positive forces, a skillful journalist can use them to advantage in gaining information.

Why does someone want to be interviewed? The reasons are many. Sometimes people will talk freely simply out of need for recognition and desire for self-esteem, status, or approval. This need for recognition is satisfied by attention from others outside their immediate circle. People are often flattered because their opinions have been solicited and because they believe in the value of the information they are giving. Thus, they feel unique and special in the eyes of those around them. So complimented, such individuals are willing to perform in exchange for recognition and other social prestige and rewards. Aware of the situation, a wise interviewer will take advantage, priming the person questioned with sincere recognition and direct praise that will have a positive effect on the interview.

Another reason some people are willing to talk can be found in the human need to identify with a higher value or cause other than immediate self-interest. For example, GI's protesting the Vietnam situation were willing to volunteer information and give testimony that was obviously painful or would jeopardize their military careers because they felt it would be of value in ending an immoral war. Likewise, caught up in circumstances that make them feel powerless, people may be tempted to "go public" in response to values they have internalized. On the day-to-day level, most people are willing to air gripes and verbalize hostility, guilt and frustration if given the opportunity and a sympathetic ear.

Sometimes people obtain release from unpleasant emotional tension by talking about past events. For example, the liberal history professor whose colleague was fired during the McCarthy loyalty hearings may feel guilty for not helping an innocent friend and may want to talk about it. If an interviewer understands or is sympathetic to these values, the knowledge can be useful in forming a strategy and set of questions that will aid in obtaining the desired information.

Often, in the final analysis, the success or failure of an interview may hinge on the expectations of the person asking the questions and this person's ability to communicate the general expectation of cooperation. This means that an interviewer must project harmony in what he or she says and feels. Asking for cooperation can be very different from expecting it. The first is verbal communication, the second is mostly nonverbal. For example, the less experienced interviewer, visibly nervous, lacking confidence and unable to focus on the importance of the task, will often ask only verbally for the information, all the while communicating nonverbally the doubt that it will be obtained. The overall effect of the verbal-nonverbal conflict is to cancel and neutralize the positive forces.

So how do you gain confidence and make use of such positive forces? The answer is through experience. But it's a lot easier if the experience is mostly successful in the beginning. So start with an easy assignment. Once you've got the basics down and your skill and self-assurance have increased, take on a more difficult assignment. You'll find projection of self-confidence an important positive force in any interview.

Worknotes
Be straight about who you are: Don't conceal your identity or the purpose of your visit. Often you will find people are as interested in you as you are in them. Talking about your assignment briefly may turn out to be a great opener and verbal exchange. Just don't get carried away and forget who is being interviewed.

In a pinch, give the impression that you have a right to know: Sometimes a good legal aid lawyer or the ACLU is useful in providing leverage on public bureaucracies. Don't go looking for trouble -- but don't
be brushed off easily. Be persistent. In the end, it pays off time and
again. If you come up against a wall, a quick call to the boss may be
useful. Then, you can always return and say, "Dr. So and So, the
Mayor, or Mrs. Smith the supervisor said it was okay if we talk."

Direct questions go a long way: They often result in direct answers.
Be up front. Don't ask, "We wonder if you might have a spare second
to give us an opinion...." Rather, "What do you think about...?"
And remember to keep the questions short. Ask three short questions
rather than a single long complicated one. Don't forget, the person
doing the interview isn't the one making the statement.

Be ready with follow-up questions: Have the counter questions to the
obvious or easy answers.   Public figures and politicians have been
asked their positions on controversial issues a hundred times. If you
do get a bite -- persist with follow-ups. Often what people will say
publicly and what they really know to be true are totally different.

Give the impression that you know more than you really do: Or give
the impression that you've alternative ways of obtaining information.
It's not necessary to make threats. Politicians know you have access to public information or can turn to the opposite camp. Often
they may be induced to tell their side if a reporter asks questions
which appear to be based on wrong information. Faced with the possibility of bad publicity, they may well tell the truth out of fear the
wrong impression will be published.

Old-fashioned persistence: Don't let the subject get away without
giving you the facts -- or a flat refusal to discuss the issue. Very
often a flat refusal to talk is the news itself.

Telephone interviews are tough: Remember, the party at the other
end can always hang up, so be direct and to the point. A telephone
interview is usually unexpected. Keep in mind that you have also
probably interrupted a person's daily schedule. When you do receive
cooperation, don't forget that a sincere thank you is in order.

Tape recorders: Tape recorders can be a real help -- or a real
hindrance. At times the tape recorder may present more
complications than it is worth. The intrusion of the machine may
cause hostile or reluctant sources to clam up. Recording interviews
presents the added burden of editing tapes, a time-consuming and
cumbersome process.

Written notes: Taking notes in an interview may also cause problems.
Writing while asking questions may put another kink in an already
awkward situation. If you interview someone unaccustomed to talking
with newspeople, try to take notes as unobtrusively as possible.
Use self-assurance, tact, politeness and genuine respect for your
source's personal integrity to calm your subject's fears of being
interviewed.

IV
Leaflets and Newsletters

Probably the single most important aspect commonly overlooked in the preparation of a leaflet or newsletter is graphic appeal. The use of bold headlines, cartoons, graphics and even halftoned photographs somewhat complicates the construction of a leaflet in the beginning. But in the long run, good graphics are worth the extra effort. For many people it's these eye-catchers which determine whether the message is read and absorbed -- or ignored.

Let's take a second, closer look at some of the examples of leaflets introduced previously in Chapter One. Studying first the example on page 44 -- Is There A Tax Credit Hiding In Your Attic? -- one is struck immediately by how well this simple leaflet stands out by itself, poster fashion. Yet a closer inspection shows the body portion of the text is cleverly divided into three distinct thirds: the graphic cartoon at the top, the informational body of type in the center and finally, the cut-out response portion at the bottom. This, of course is deliberate; the leaflet was designed not only to be tacked on wallboards, but to be folded and stuffed in envelopes together with a utility bill. Thus,

"H'MM... THEIR 3 COLOR LAYOUT IS QUITE DYNAMIC."

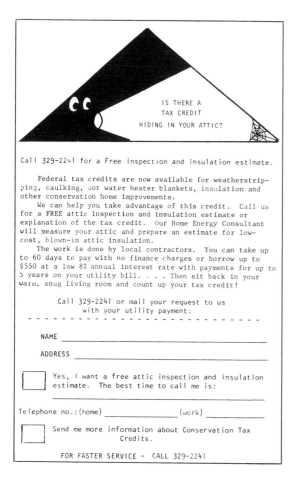

Call 329-2241 for a Free inspection and insulation estimate.

Federal tax credits are now available for weatherstripping, caulking, hot water heater blankets, insulation and other conservation home improvements.

We can help you take advantage of this credit. Call us for a FREE attic inspection and insulation estimate or explanation of the tax credit. Our Home Energy Consultant will measure your attic and prepare an estimate for low-cost, blown-in attic insulation.

The work is done by local contractors. You can take up to 60 days to pay with no finance charges or borrow up to $550 at a low 8% annual interest rate with payments for up to 5 years on your utility bill. . . . Then sit back in your warm, snug living room and count up your tax credit!

Call 329-2241 or mail your request to us
with your utility payment:

NAME _____

ADDRESS _____

[ ] Yes, I want a free attic inspection and insulation
estimate. The best time to call me is:
_____

Telephone no.:(home) _____ (work) _____

[ ] Send me more information about Conservation Tax
Credits.

FOR FASTER SERVICE - CALL 329-2241

upon opening the envelope the reader first encounters the cartoon and then, hopefully, is invited into unfolding it further and reading the typed copy. Then, at the bottom a response section to be torn off and returned is provided. Notice also how the telephone number is prominently displayed in all three sections of this leaflet.

Leaflet Construction

Let's take a closer look at the construction of another leaflet on the following page. This was used successfully in a union organizing effort. Many times leaflets are calls to action and this example is no exception. The second in a series of three, this leaflet was a fast way of informing a lot of people about an immediate situation: in this instance, a pending grievance. In addition, it was a persuasive organizing tool, demonstrating the need for a union and asking workers to vote for the union in the upcoming election.

Printed on purple paper using an offset press, this example measures 8 1/2" x 11". Headlines were done with rub-off lettering (page 79) and the master typed on an IBM Selectric typewriter (page 93) using two different balls or fonts, one standard, the other italic. The two other leaflets in the series were similarly laid out, but printed on different color paper, one on golden yellow, the other on bright green. The different colors help people distinguish one leaflet from the next. In

JULIA HARVEY DENIED JOB
— MONEY IS AVAILABLE

It was disclosed recently that enough money was offered to the Dept. of Pediatrics to pay Julia Harvey's salary indefinitely. But in a direct reversal of what he said last Dec. 29, Dr. Schulman, Dept. head, is now refusing to accept money offered through the laboratory at the Children's Hospital at Stanford in order to keep the 60 year old research assistant on the University payroll. Schulman had written Julia:

"Since support for your position is now totally dependent upon the funds (from the lab at the Children's Hospital) and since the amount now on hand is sufficient for only a three month period, the extension of your appointment will be until March 31, 1973. Should additional funds become available to Dr. Robertson's laboratory at the Children's Hospital at Stanford or for his research program, your appointment may, of course be extended further . . ."

GRIEVANCE IS FILED

Now money is available. Even though this is so, after 25 years at Stanford, Ms. Harvey was terminated March 31 of this year. Prior to her layoff, she and USE Asst. President Jan Sutter filed a formal grievance with Emil Sarpa, Director of Personnel. As Julia's representative, Jan had this to say:

"This is simply the latest in a series of procedural atrocities and violations of University policy pertaining to the layoff and re-employment of Ms. Harvey. In the first place, Ms. Harvey's original layoff was in violation of Stanford policy. Next, a research position fell vacant in the department for which she was completely qualified. Pediatrics was compelled by the Stanford Guidelines to give Ms. Harvey employment preference. This it failed to do. Further, Pediatrics violated policy when it filled the position with a person less qualified. It was negligent when it failed to post the position.

Now, along comes an offer from the Children's Hospital, where Julia does her research, to fund her work. What does Schulman do? He won't accept the money!"

CAN PEDIATRICS VIOLATE STANFORD POLICY?

You'd think the Dean's office would put a quick end to such double dealing. Yet after 2 hours of patient explanation, Richard Balch, Associate Dean for the Administration, refused to enforce the University Guidelines. This denial of elementary justice came even as a surprise to us.

WHERE FROM HERE?

Julia and Jan are taking the grievance to outside arbitration before a non-University hearing officer. This is the final resort. In all likelihood, Julia will win her job back -- but only with an incredible effort on her part and only with the help of USE.

WHAT ABOUT THE REST OF US?

Few of us could have put up as determined a fight as Julia Harvey. But each of us can do something to protect ourselves. We can support USE Local 680, AFL-CIO, in fighting unfair management practices. This June 6, 1600 of us vote for union representation. Julia Harvey is living proof of why we need a union.

Julia Harvey pickets to retain her job outside the office of Dean Clayton Rich.

Medical Center Committee to support Julia Harvey. USE Local 680, S.E.I.U. AFL-CIO.

addition, when tacked up on cluttered bulletin boards, the bright colors help them stand out. The photograph was taken earlier on a protest picketline and then halftoned (page 86) at the printers. In a pinch, had no screening camera been available, the original photo could have been covered with plastic 60-line-per-inch dot screen and pasted to the flat.

In the leaflet, the bold headlines, the colored paper and the photograph are used as hooks to get the reader interested in the text. Likewise, the broken paragraphs, italicized quotes and subheads with breathing space between paragraphs are visual enticement. Notice there is no border around the photograph. Here, a border would have cluttered the overall design.

The Text

Let's take a closer look at the text of this example. Studying the copy structure, it becomes apparent that the leaflet uses a modified news story approach to illustrate a concrete problem. There's a lead paragraph with most of the five w's and the h. The body of the story follows in a quote, summary fashion. Finally, at the bottom, comes a pitch to vote for the union in an upcoming election.

One of the immediate objectives of the leaflet is to inform people about the grievance. Another is to use public leverage through the power of publicity to sway public opinion and force management to grant just demands. A third might be to lay the groundwork for direct action -- like another protest picket line, a work stoppage or slowdown. Regardless, all are

Open or "white" space is the thing to note in all of these examples. Observe how the eye appeal of each is enhanced by leaving much of the area of the leaflet blank. Sometimes beginners try to jam together too much copy or use too many graphics -- techniques which confuse the eye. These examples, however, nicely illustrate the correct use of white space.

short-run tactics in a much longer strategy of winning a union election. Handed one of these, the worker can't but ponder: "After twenty-five years on the job can they do this to me? Without a union contract and binding arbitration, I have no protection. Here's management violating its own policy and procedures." Here are the specifics of what's happened to her: with no union, what's going to protect me?

Other Options

Going to an outside print shop is not the only way of producing a leaflet. If immediacy and money are a problem, other options are cheaper, faster and more versatile than offset printing. For anything

The Buffalo Bulletin. This newsletter was produced using an electrostencil and mimeograph machine. Newsletters differ from leaflets in that they usually are more than one page long and contain a selection of information arranged most often in order of descending importance. Notice how the editor has maintained lots of white space while still packing the copy in.

The Fat City Outrage~Express

and P.A.T.U. NEWS

October 1973
vol. II. no. 5

RENT CONTROL

Rent and eviction control will be on the ballot next spring, depending on when we finish gathering the required 4,100 signatures on the two petitions. We already have 2,700 and are shooting for 3,000 more to compensate for any that the Registrar declares invalid. We will be hitting the supermarkets again where we expect to collect about 12 per hour. Give Bill Lane a call at 32-4972 to help with a two-hour shift.

The landlords are already running scared because they know that our rent and eviction control laws were designed for the tenant—not the landlord as is the case with most housing laws. And they know that if we collect 5,000 signatures or more, that may be enough voters to win the election right there. So the Tri-County Apartment Association has put out a request for contributions for the anti-rent control campaign (e.g., "Rent control breeds rats"). Meanwhile, a questionnaire mailed to all

residents of Fire Zone 1 in downtown Palo Alto shows that 87% favor rent control.

But rent control has had a legal setback in Berkeley. The rent control law which the voters passed by the initiative process was struck down by the courts last August. The City is appealing, and it instituted a rent freeze for forty-five days, ending October 1. The City Council wasn't interested in continuing with the freeze and now October rent increases are hitting Berkeley tenants. The Berkeley Tenants Organizing Committee is calling a mass meeting to protest these rent increases and to encourage tenants to withhold rents until their landlord agrees to negotiate a rental contract with their building tenant union. Presently there are rent strikes by some tenants who are demanding less rents, more repairs, and the right to control rent money to make repairs and manage their buildings themselves.

—Brad Dowden
—John Roger

FIRE ZONE 1

Fire Zone 1 is an area in downtown Palo Alto which includes the University Avenue shopping district and the surrounding neighborhood. In 1946 the city established a commercial fire zone which required that buildings be made of noncombustible materials such as concrete and steel to reduce the risk of fire in closely spaced businesses. (This was part of the trend to develop downtown Palo Alto into a major commercial center.) Owners of wood frame buildings, most of which were homes, were prohibited from making repairs and alterations on their buildings. As a result, the condition of these homes deteriorated. These moves by the City paved the way for the demolition of 101 units in Fire Zone I between 1960 and 1970, and for the proposal by Palo Alto's fire chief that all wooden structures in Fire Zone I be demolished within 15 years. Even so, there are still about 400 housing units left in Fire Zone I, housing about 700 people.

Last year the City Council directed the staff to study Fire Zone I and to devise ways to "preserve and enhance" its residential structures. Last March the city brought together a group of people interested in the fire zone to advise the staff in their study. PATU participated in this group even though it was heavily loaded with landlords, property owners and representatives of commercial interests. We hoped that we could prevail on the city staff to follow the Council's directive to give special attention to those "disadvantaged in the housing market." (continued on last page)

Fat City Outrage-Express. A second sample of an 8 1/2" x 14" newsletter done with electrostencil and mimeograph machine. Notice how well the line drawings are reproduced and how the authors took care not to crowd the headlines or banner at the top of the page.

up to five thousand copies, a wise way to proceed is to use an electrostencil cutting machine like a Gestetner to cut a mimeograph stencil and roll off the required leaflets at about a third the offset cost. There is some loss in the quality of reproduction using a mimeograph, but if done with care, the electrostencil method approaches offset quality and will render headlines, cartoons and drawings excellently. Even photographs will reproduce satisfactorily if the original is screened and the mimeograph lightly inked. The above is a good example of what can be produced using the electrostencil-mimeograph combination.

Newsletters

Newsletters differ from simple leaflets in several ways. Usually they are longer, often more than one page, and each edition may deal with a number of topics ranging from crisis issues to trivia. The Buffalo Bulletin from Service Employees Local 715 illustrates some of the basic qualities of a good newsletter. Mimeographed, using an electrostenciled master, the original Bulletin measures 8 1/2" x 14". It has a consistent banner featuring the local's mascot buffalo. The buffalo is important for membership recognition when the newsletter is tacked on bulletin boards or handed out. Notice how the editor has arranged the copy in order of descending importance. This particular issue was done using an IBM Selectric typewriter and rub-off headlines. It's also probably safe to assume that the editor was both in a hurry and tight for copy space when this was produced, as one valid criticism of the lack of columns on the front pages is that the reader is very likely to feel overwhelmed by the sea of grey type. Yet even so, while jamming in an incredible amount of text, the editor took pains to at least leave lots of white space around the buffalo, between the headlines and in various areas on the second page.

Another way of doing a newsletter is in a booklet format such as illustrated by the Housing Hotline on page 50. This uses standard 8 1/2" x 14" paper, but folds it once in the center, sideways, making a little booklet. By using this method, the front and back pages are contained together on the same sheet of paper, while the inside pages are printed on the reverse side. One advantage to the booklet format is that it makes the newsletter easier to handle and hand out than the long sheets unfolded. The leaflet on page 51 uses the same format. Here, though, the example is a professionally printed job, employing justified type where both the right and left margins of typed copy are perfectly even. Incidentally, it's important to note here that for illustration purposes the front and back pages of both the booklet examples have been reversed left for right. The actual front page of both newsletters is on the right side of the page.

HOUSING HOTLINE

HOUSING COALITION Of San Mateo Co. April 1980

Phony 'Fair Rent' Bill

NO on 10

The Housing Coalition is urging a No vote to defeat Proposition 10, the phony 'Fair Rent' initiative on the June ballot. This measure, if passed, will invalidate every rent relief ordinance now in force anywhere in the state of California, In addition, it's been called an outright 'fraud', 'sham' and 'deception' by the Los Angeles Times. In fact, so heated has been the protest, that even Howard Jarvis, who originally backed this bill, is getting cold feet as cries of voter fraud mount up.

As the Times editorial of January 2 points out, Prop 10 is so full of double-talk that it had even confused the people circulating the petitions on its behalf in to thinking it would lower rents and protect them from gouging. But the case

---

Los Angeles Times

HARRISON GRAY OTIS, 1882-1917
HARRY CHANDLER, 1917-1944
NORMAN CHANDLER, 1944-1960

NO on 10

HOUSING COALITION Of San Mateo Co.

4 Part II WEDNESDAY, JANUARY 2, 1980

Newspeak or Realspeak?

Newspeak is the language of counterfeit politics that George Orwell invented for manipulating minds in his novel, "1984." In newspeak, left is right and suffering is the only true joy.

Newspeak unfortunately has appeared often in real life, but never in as pure a form as in a campaign for an initiative that seems certain to appear on the ballot in June under the title, "Rent control." Actually, it is designed to hobble rent control.

The campaign is supported by a coalition of landlords and construction workers through an organization known as Californians for Fair Rent. In newspeak, that is high rents.

The deception is so complete that Times reporters recently found a young man gathering signatures on petitions, at 30 cents a name, who seemed to genuinely believe that had it been approved earlier it would have helped him fight off a recent increase in his own rent. Obviously, he had not read the petition that he was carrying around.

We have always opposed rent control, partly for reasons of principle but largely because it does more harm than good in the long run by discouraging investment in the only place that can stabilize rents—new housing.

But we feel at least as strongly about fraud, particularly when its target is the basic legal document of the state, the Constitution, and when the subject is one as intensely felt as shelter. In such circumstances, newspeak is a dangerous game.

There is little doubt that the initiative will qualify. More than 1 million people signed petitions, and something more than half a million would have been enough.

There is also little doubt that few of the people who signed the petitions read beyond the words "Rent control."

Times reporters found one person gathering signatures by asking passersby, "Would you like to sign our petition for lower rent in California?" Who could refuse?

But, had the passerby read the entire text, he would have found that rents would rise faster than the costs of owning property under the formula in the initiative.

Rents would keep pace with the consumer price index, which goes up faster than the price of paint or light bulbs or a landlord's mortgage payments—which alone represent half the cost of owning rental property.

The initiative would dismantle all rent-control machinery now in place anywhere in the state, and would make it unconstitutional for the state government to involve itself in controls.

New rent-control ordinances would require approval in a referendum.

Actually, voters in California have shown good judgement when the rent-control issue has been put on the ballot. With some exceptions, most such proposals have been voted down, most recently in El Monte.

Whether voters, particularly older renters squeezed to the point of tears by inflation, would keep smiling through a sham like the fair-rent initiative is another question. The more likely outcome would be a backlash and a counterinitiative that would make existing rent-control ordinances look good to landlords.

We hope the proposition fails in June. Then, we hope, the coalition of property owners and construction workers will come back with a proposal that guarantees landlords enough profit to make rental housing a good investment.

We would be delighted to support that kind of realspeak. □

NO on 10

PHONY RENT INITIATIVE

is, Prop 10 will do just the opposite. In fact, many of the people signing the petitions are now suing to have their names removed. Meanwhile, a full 42% of the names on the qualifying petitions -- an all time high -- have been invalidated. Unfortunately, Prop 10 still qualified for the ballot.

What is Proposition 10?

Prop 10 is a constitutional amendment that will greatly restrict a local government's ability to enact any sort of meaningful rent control. In addition, it's clearly inflationary, unfair to the tenant, discriminatory, and in parts, probably a violation of a citizen's rights of due process as guaranteed by the State and Federal constitutions.

-- Prop 10 voids all rent control measures now in effect throughout the state. Even those enacted by a direct vote of the people. It makes it unconstitutional for the state to involve itself in rent control. In addition, it gives a blanket exemption to single unit dwellings (35% of all rental housing), regardless of whether a landlord owns 1 or 250 such housing units.

-- Prop 10 is unfair to the tenant because it allows the landlord to even illegally hike rents and evict a tenant who refuses or is unable to pay the increase. Then, under the Prop 10 vacancy decontrol provisions, the landlord can re-rent the housing at a higher rate and the tenant has no legal recourse. This is because in the fine print, Prop 10 specifically provides that non-payment of rent can not be used as an eviction defense.

-- It will discourage the construction of new housing units which we so desperately need in San Mateo County. This is because, according to an anlysis by the California State Department of Housing and Community Development, it may prohibit or regulate such encouragements as density bonus permits or housing built on land sold at a written down cost by state or local government.

NO on 10

HOUSING COALITION Of San Mateo Co.

--It's inflationary because it mandates that a landlord receive a guaranteed annual rent increase equal to or in many instances greater than the rise in the consumer price index. It forces expensive and unnecessary elections, adding to our taxes.

-- Perhaps even more important its voter fraud and manipulation of the election process. Calling Prop 10 'Newspeak' and the 'language of counterfeit politics ... for manipulating minds' the Los Angeles Times goes on to say, '...we feel at least as strongly about fraud, particularly when its target is the basis document of the state, the Constitution, and when the subject is one as intensely felt as shelter.'

HOUSING COALITION Of San Mateo Co

2615 Fair Oaks Ave.
Redwood City, Ca. 94063

PHONE NUMBERS ARE: 369-8249 369-4457 366-1877

Next time your rent goes up, why not do something about it? The Housing Coalition is the only organization in San Mateo County fighting for tenant's rights. As a membership group, we need you to sustain us both with volunteer work and money. Annual dues are $5 for individuals, $10 for organizations. If you're really hurting, there's a special $2 rate for low income.

NAME ____________________ PHONE ________

ADDRESS ____________________

I am enclosing $ ____ to support the Housing Coalition

2615 Fair Oaks Avenue, Redwood City, Ca. 94063

WE OPPOSE THE HOLIDAY INN BECAUSE IT WILL:

- STIMULATE FURTHER OVER-DEVELOPMENT IN PALO ALTO

- RAISE TAXES AND RENTS BY SPURRING INCREASED PROPERTY TAX ASSESSMENTS

- YIELD FAR SMALLER FINANCIAL BENEFITS TO THE CITY THAN THE DEVELOPER CLAIMS

GIVE THE DEVELOPERS AND SPECULATORS A CLEAR MESSAGE

VOTE NO

PROPOSITION K   JUNE 6

WHAT'S THE BIG PICTURE?

The plans of large corporate developers only explains part of the move by Holiday Inn to build in Palo Alto. The other is explained by the nature of the corporation itself. The Holiday Inn is a huge conglomerate which is expanding everywhere, literally scouring the world in search for profits. It has assets of $575 million dollars and is the largest company in the lodging industry. In addition to owning its own construction company, it has its own bus lines, computer company, hotel supply company, food company and many other subsidiaries.

As a giant corporation Holiday Inn has no concern for the people of Palo Alto or anywhere else for that matter. Palo Alto is merely one of the Holiday Inn's targets. Nor does it confine its activities to the U.S. alone. It is continuing to exploit the beaches, mountains, and cultures of such places as the Dominican Republic, Puerto Rico, Mexico and Morroco. Chen, the co-developer of the Holiday Inn in Palo Alto, is also working to build two Holiday Inns in Cambodia. An example of Chen's lack of concern for the communities in which he builds his hotels is the 27 story blockbuster he built in a low-income area of Chinatown despite overwhelming community opposition and a severe housing problem.

THE HOLIDAY INN IS A TEST CASE FOR FUTURE DEVELOPMENT.

VOTE NO   PROPOSITION K

SEND MUCH NEEDED CONTRIBUTIONS TO: PALO ALTO TENANTS' UNION
                                      611 WEBSTER STREET
                                      PALO ALTO, CALIFORNIA 94301

TO HELP WITH CANVASSING, DISTRIBUTING LEAFLETS, OR FOR FURTHER INFORMATION CALL: 321-7387 or 324-4872 or 329-7418.

WE ARE OPPOSED TO THE CONSTRUCTION OF A MULTI-MILLION DOLLAR 280-ROOM HOLIDAY INN IN DOWNTOWN PALO ALTO.

DOES PALO ALTO NEED ANOTHER HOTEL?

Definitely Not. Vacancy rates have remained at 35% for over a year. Another 200 room hotel has already been approved at Dillingham's Palo Alto Square. Although Palo Alto has a surplus of existing and planned hotel units, we have a severe housing crisis. Vacancy rates stand at below 1%.

WHO WANTS IT?

In spite of these facts corporate business interests are working for the hotel. Like the defeated Superblock, the Holiday Inn is part of an attempt to turn Palo Alto into a regional financial and industrial center. A newspaper ad for Dillingham's Palo Alto Square stated "A wooded wallstreet is going up in Palo Alto."

WHAT'S AT STAKE?

New pressures for overdevelopment hinge on the outcome of this election. The developers (Stanford) of the proposed Palo Alto Plaza (two high rise office towers on the Mayfield School site across from Palo Alto Square) have postponed their request for a zoning change until after the June 6 election. They want to see what the political climate for development is. Likewise the formal announcement of plans to revive efforts to build a hospital in downtown Palo Alto is also being postponed until after the Holiday Inn election. In addition to these immediate threats the Inn would provide the kind of facilities needed to induce major corporate headquarters to locate in Palo Alto, creating pressure for more office buildings.

WILL THE CITY BENEFIT?

The developer's major selling points for the Holiday Inn are the supposed financial benefits. But city revenue projections are based on a 70% occupancy rate. However, the city motel market is already glutted. Thus:

- The revenue projections are inflated.
- Since Palo Alto's present lodgings accommodate all its visitors (38% vacancy rate) the city revenues gained from the Holiday Inn will be lost from other small hotels.
- The Holiday Inn profits will come only with accelerated commercial growth, the kind of growth that Palo Alto residents have rejected in the last three elections.
- Once built the hotel will serve the self fulfilling function of stimulating further large commercial development.

- By allowing city land to be used for a major hotel development, the city itself would become tied to the profitability of the development. The city, therefore, would assume a vested interest in approving further developments which would attempt to assure full occupancy of the Holiday Inn.

WHAT ARE THE HIDDEN COSTS?

Any small financial benefits will be eroded by higher costs to Palo Alto residents. The city will be responsible for installing utilities, modifying access roads, and providing other services. With other development planned for the area major city wide expenditures will be necessary such as a new expressway on Alma, another attempt at the Willow Freeway, and an underpass expansion under El Camino and Page Mill Road.

WHERE DOES IT ALL LEAD?

Increased development, widening and construction of roadways and freeways increases Palo Alto's development potential and drives up land values. They in turn drive up property taxes and rents. This generates a vicious cycle whereby property tax increases become so steep they drive small homeowners and tenants out of the city. Land is then put to more intensive use–housing is demolished, expensive apartments and high rises take their place, and the process is repeated all over again. Unless we break this cycle, Palo Alto will be turned into a city dominated by luxury apartments, concrete and steel high rises, and plastic hotels.

ARE THERE ADVERSE SOCIAL EFFECTS?

Along with planned overdevelopment comes more water and air pollution, and general environmental decay that is already having a destructive effect on Palo Alto. Using city money and resources to give special advantages to a multi national corporation such as Holiday Inn means that social needs go largely unmet. The city is giving the use of land which is a public resource to a private developer. The developers will use it to further their own private gain while the community need for housing will be worsened.

WILL EMPLOYMENT INCREASE?

Not significantly. Since the corporation has its own construction company, there is no guarantee that local contractors or construction workers will benefit. Up to 80 people may work there, but because the Inn will be pushing other smaller hotels out of business, it won't substantially increase the number of jobs in this area. The kind of jobs it offers are dead end, low wage jobs, not the kind of jobs that make it possible for people to live decent lives.

Worknotes

The fastest, cheapest and
most effective way to get a
leaflet out in a hurry is to use an
electrostencil and mimeograph.
Study religiously the manual for
both machines and find someone
who can show you how to work them.
Clean the mimeograph thoroughly and go light
on the ink. Stay away from the cheapest grades
of mimeo paper with their atrociously dull colors.

Up to a thousand leaflets can be turned out in a few hours for less
than $20 using this combination. Many churches, schools and commu-
nity organizations have mimeographs. For less than a dollar a side, a
print shop will burn an electrostencil.   Another option is to rent the
electrostencil cutting machine on a monthly basis.

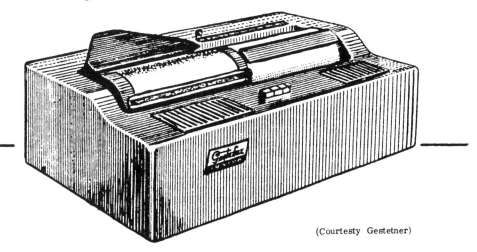

(Courtesty Gestetner)

V
Newspapers

Small newspapers present a challenge in composition and design compared to a simple leaflet or newsletter. For one thing, there is a lot more copy to deal with. For another, the makeup demands of an eight- or sixteen-page paper -- where articles, ads, photos and headlines all compete for the reader's eye -- are understandably complex.

Format

Perhaps format is a good place to begin our discussion of newspapers. Format is the term used to describe the general appearance of a newspaper, newsletter or leaflet. It has to do with such things as page size, number of columns and the way the columns are separated. Keep in mind that most of the principles discussed here apply to newsletters and leaflets as well.

Small newspapers such as those published by student and community groups often use what is known as a tabloid format. A tabloid page measures about 11" x 14" and contains from three to five columns. Large daily papers, in contrast, contain eight or more columns and are twice the size of a "tab" paper. Nor is a tabloid paper just a scaled-down version of a standard newspaper. Whereas a conventional paper often approximates a crazy quilt, the tab has a more straightforward look, many times resembling that of a magazine.

There are many advantages to the tabloid format, not the least of which is its smaller size, making it easy for the reader to handle and comprehend. The layout is simplified too. On a single page, it is often the case that three or four substantial articles are all that are

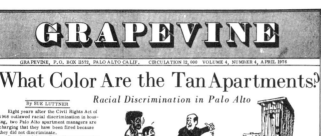

GRAPEVINE

GRAPEVINE, P.O. BOX 11572, PALO ALTO CALIF.   CIRCULATION 12,000   VOLUME 4, NUMBER 4, APRIL 1976

What Color Are the Tan Apartments?

Racial Discrimination in Palo Alto

By SUE LUTTNER

Eight years after the Civil Rights Act of 1968 outlawed racial discrimination in housing, two Palo Alto apartment managers are charging that they have been fired because they did not discriminate.

Pamela and Jerry Donnelly are now taking their case to court in an effort to put an end to what they consider discrimination by the Youritan Construction Company. The "Tan" apartments include approximately 1,000 units in several complexes scattered about Palo Alto. The Donnellys managed the Tan Village complex, bordering Amarillo in south Palo Alto, from July 1975 until this February.

In an affidavit regarding her and her husband's employment by Tan, Pamela said: "On numerous occasions we were expected to tell minorities there were not vacancies that really existed, direct them to certain sections of apartments, apply different standards of income evaluation, treat them different than whites when rent payments were late, delay needed apartment repairs and improvements when minority tenants requested them."

James Wolpman, a lawyer for the Donnellys, called this behavior "second level discrimination," which he said is harder to prove than open hostility.

Tan's attorney Neil Falconer told the GRAPEVINE, "Our client does not discriminate." He also said that Tan had "good and sufficient reasons" for discharging the Donnellys.

Pamela and Jerry started working for Tan last summer. At the time, Pamela was given a statement to sign, saying she would not discriminate on basis of race. This requirement stemmed from a 1971 court decision against Tan, in which the company was enjoined from discriminating. In that case, complaints by tenants and prospective renters and a check by teams from the Midpeninsula Citizens for Fair Housing (MCFH) convicted the court that Tan had been practicing discrimination.

MCFH is never directly involved in law suits, but it coordinated a check in which black couples and white couples applied for apartments at close to the same time. The check five years ago revealed significantly different treatment. In 1971, only 14 of the 1133 units owned by Tan were rented by blacks. The reporting requirement contained in the injunction expired this February.

Pamela listed in the affidavit specific incidents in which minorities seemed to receive different treatment than whites:
• A man from Tel Aviv was told that only one apartment was vacant when there were

(continued on page 2)

'I've got just the thing for you boys, a cosy back cabin. There will be $150 cleaning deposit - plus first and last month's rent.'

Growth of Nuclear Power Industry Could Fuel Atom Bomb Terrorism

By JOSHUA GOLDSTEIN

New York (April 1, 1977) - Federal police and civil defense workers, exhausted from four days of frenzied work, today completed the evacuation of New York City's population hours ahead of the scheduled detonation of an atomic bomb hidden somewhere in the city. Police called off a fruitless search for the device, built by the terrorist Black September organization using Uranium-235 hijacked from a truck carrying materials from a West German nuclear power plant.

A communique from the terrorists last week warned that the atomic bomb, of Hiroshima size, would explode tonight in New York in retaliation for stepped-up U.S. military support to Israel in the Mideast war. However, the evacuation did not proceed until five days ago when the terrorists exploded "Bomb #1" in the Arizona desert to show they meant business. The terrorists had evaded an unprecedented international police search following the uranium hijack.

President Jackson announced an indefinite extension of the National State of Emergency, ordering continued mass arrests of suspected radicals...

April Fool? Maybe not.

The growth of the nuclear power industry over the rest of this century will bring with it an unprecedented proliferation of fissionable materials -- the stuff atom bombs are made from. The technical knowledge needed to make these materials explode, once top-secret, is now openly available in public documents and textbooks. Given a small amount of nuclear material, the cost of producing an atomic bomb capable of destroying a city could be as low as $1000; it could be assembled in a two-car garage. The past record in handling nuclear materials indicates that security is, and may always be, imperfect.

A growing number of nuclear experts consider "homemade" atomic bombs a very real and immediate danger -- one which the public knows too little about. The Curve of Binding Energy by John McPhee (with Theodore Taylor, an ex-designer of atomic bombs for the U.S. government), and Nuclear Theft: Risks and Safeguards, by Taylor and Mason

(continued on page 8)

WHAT'S INSIDE

The GRAPEVINE is a visually balanced, relatively simple example of what is possible with an offset tabloid newspaper. Note how it uses a three-column format, giving the paper something of a magazine appearance.

printed. The result is something of a departmentalization which can be put to great advantage. Unlike conventional papers, tabs can devote whole pages to consistent topics, themes or even single articles in an in-depth fashion.

The front page of the GRAPEVINE, above, demonstrates quite well some of these characteristics of the tabloid style format. The community newspaper uses three-column format, giving it a magazine-like appearance. And since the newspaper uses "strike on" typesetting directly from an IBM Executive typewriter, it has a ragged right margin. The "alleys" or areas between columns are left unruled. This helps to give white space relief. So does the generous white space left around the headlines and cartoon.

The GRAPEVINE nameplate or banner at the top of the front page and the double ruled lines around the edge of the paper give it something of a poster quality. Notice, too, this community newspaper has only two articles sharing the front page area.

For the first century and a half of publishing, newspaper editors pretty much relied on intuition when drawing up the front page. More recently a few guidelines have been established. Studies show that the eye naturally tends to focus on certain areas of a page. One of these areas is the optical center -- not to be confused with the geometric center. This optical center is located about two inches above the geometrical center and slightly to the right. In our example, the three cartoon figures demonstrate good use of this phenomenon.

The second area that the eye tends to go to is the upper left corner. From years of habit, our mind tells us to hit out for the upper left of any printed item because that's the beginning. From here, it slowly makes its way down the bottom, terminating in the right corner. This leaves two areas that have a lesser drawing power. They are the upper right and lower left corners. In the examples the lower left corner is the lone-

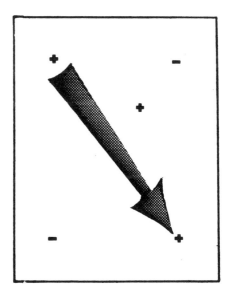

liest portion of the page. From all this is derived a general guideline: anything placed in the primary optical areas -- with the optical center and the upper left being the biggest drawers -- is more likely to be read and comprehended. Conversely, getting the reader's eye into the upper right and lower left corners is comparatively more difficult.

The lower diagram on the preceding page illustrates this principle, the crosses pointing out the primary optical areas and the minus signs the areas where the eye is less likely to fall. Additionally, the large arrow indicates how the eye generally tends to travel down the page in a diagonal fashion.

Once explained, it's easy to see a lot of this at work in our example front page. The first thing to note is the placement of the cartoon smack in the optical center of the page. Then observe how the primary headline begins in the upper left-hand corner of the page and the secondary headline falls on a diagonal below it, corresponding exactly to the direction of eye travel as indicated by the arrow in the lower diagram.

In addition to what we have already discussed, there is another phenomenon at work here also. Notice how the cartoon apartment manager's hand acts as an arrow or line of force, pushing the eye in the direction of the upper right-hand corner.   These lines of force are something to pay attention to, and are contained to some degree in all photographs and illustrations. For example, a speeding locomotive will compel us to look in the direction of its travel. A pointed revolver will cause the eye to seek out its intended victim. Similarly, lines of force are established by the direction a subject is looking in a photograph. Thus an old rule validly says that photos should face into the page. Arrows, pointed hands, potential and actual projections, the sweep of a dress -- all set up lines of force which propel the eyes.   The trick is to harness this influence and use it to interest the reader and channel the eye into the body of copy.

An awareness of the primary optical areas and lines of force caused the cartoon to be placed where it was. The effect upon the eye is interesting. Drawn to the cartoon character's hand, one's eye tends to loop

upward and to the left top corner where the main headline begins.
Then, following the invisible diagonal arrow, it falls on the second
headline, finally dropping to the bottom right corner where waiting
nearby in the center column is a small index titled "What's Inside."
The overall effect is worth studying, because in this example, just
about anywhere the eye happens to strike on the page, it tends to be
drawn into the body of copy.

As a test of the theory, try to imagine the visual catastrophe
if the nuclear article and the cartoon were simply switched. Not
only would the headlines bump, but a casual reader would be discouraged by the forbidding mass of copy. Meanwhile, the badly
located cartoon figure down in the lower right corner would be directing the reader's eye towards the never-never land beyond his
right elbow.

From all this we begin to see that most important in the design
of a front page is the provision of a strong attention incentive. In
the example it was the large cartoon. Of course the purpose of
such a compelling visual is to attract the reader, inducing him
to pick up the paper and dive into the copy. Knowing where the primary optical areas are goes a long way in determining where a
photo or illustration should go. Our GRAPEVINE example uses
a cartoon, but a provocative photo, especially an action shot, seems
to rank the strongest as an attention grabber.

Before we turn to the placement of copy, a few more suggestions
on front-page design are in order. One is that care should be taken
to make each front page distinctive. This means that the latest issue
should be not only different from competing publications but also as
distinct as possible from its predecessors. The reason for this is
that if a reader can't tell the latest issue from the last, it may well
not be picked up at all.

The banner or nameplate is important also. It should be distinctive, separating your publication from all the others. Usually the
nameplate is located across the top of the front page. But a "floating"

The ORACLE, a student newspaper, demonstrates the concept of a "floating" banner or nameplate. Unlike the GRAPEVINE, the banner appears here in the middle of the front page and can be adjusted up or down according to the space requirements of the copy.

Ecology Club makes its point

Hays leads Conservation Week

By GREG NERLAND

Last week marked the Ecology Club's second annual Conservation Week at Gunn High. Displays and discussions highlighted the week-long effort to introduce the idea of conservation to the students of Gunn.

The strive to conserve actually started during the week of April 27. Three digit numbers appeared daily on the roof of the library. It was later discovered that the numbers represented the amount of cars in the Gunn parking lot that day.

"It's ridiculous that we should have 400 cars in the parking lot. I could understand if it was raining, but in this nice weather, there are other ways," stated Wally Hays, president of the Ecology Club.

The planned activities of Conservation Week started on Monday, May 4 with an assembly featuring Richard Rosey of Global 2000. Global 2000 is a committee which presented an official report to ex-President Carter during his term.

On Tuesday, a number of stands were placed in center quad. The various tables presented possible solutions to food and energy problems, as well as a host of other problems facing our world.

"All we are trying to do is teach and make conservation aware to the students and faculty at Gunn," explained Hays on the purpose of Conservation Week.

Wednesday featured a group using the acronym YES (Youth Evolving Solution). YES gave a presentation under the premise of "Salvatierra" (Save the Earth).

Lunch on Thursday was highlighted with a slide show by Steven Moore. Moore, the coordinator of Palo Alto Mattertals Recovery program, talked about recycling programs in Palo Alto, both new and old. Moore stressed that dumpsites in Palo Alto are running out and we need to recycle.

According to Moore, Palo Alto has the best waste management in the United States. With curbside recycling of aluminum, glass, and a new program, wood recovery, Palo Alto is a model city for the rest of America.

Ending the talk by Moore was a slide show titled, "Running out of Room." The show revealed that Americans are pre-trained to waste.

Throughout the week, a stand had been placed in center quad offering a variety of objects with conservation themes. Everything from T-shirts with the slogan, "We the People of Palo Alto Recycle," to pads of recycled paper were available.

"We are trying to raise money to do things like insulate the water heaters," explained Kim Hatasaka, staffer at the stand.

Conservation Week wound up Friday with a solar energy display. Friday was aptly titled "Sun Day, the wonders of solar power." Solar powered cookers and lights highlighted the presentation.

Ecology Club president Wally Hays demonstrates a solar heater during a lunchtime exhibition on Sun Day, May 8.

ORACLE

Volume 17, Number 14
May 15, 1981

Henry M. Gunn Senior High School
780 Arastradero Rd., Palo Alto, CA

To succeed Harbeck as Oracle head
Farrell named advisor

By ANN VANDENBERG

English teacher Tim Farrell has been named to replace Stanford graduate student Tom Harbeck as faculty advisor to the Oracle for the 1981-1982 school year.

Farrell accepted the offer for the one-year job made by English Department Head Mary Lee Glass two weeks ago. A former football and varsity baseball coach, he is eager to return to coaching, but this time coaching journalism.

"If there was ever a year for becoming advisor of the Oracle, this is the one," Farrell says. "Many members of this year's experienced editorial staff will be coming back next year to help me through the rough spots.

Harbeck feels the staff is prepared for a new advisor since, during the last year, it has firmly established Oracle policies.

Says Harbeck, "We've cut down production time about one third from the beginning of the year. We no longer work late at night. Also, the writing quality of articles has improved."

Farrell plans few significant changes on Oracle policy next year but wants to permanently abolish working at night.

"I'm not a late-night person," he states, claiming, "We'll get up at 4:00 a.m. to work if we need to but we won't stay until midnight. We'll either work more efficiently or start production earlier."

Next year, beginning and advanced journalism classes will be combined into one seventh period class. Consequently, the beginning class will be directly involved with Oracle production without as much emphasis on traditional textbook training and simulation. However, Farrell says, both groups will do different activities at times.

Jazz Band placed on state top ten

By JIM YARDLEY

For the third consecutive year, the Gunn Jazz Band has been selected as one of the ten finalists in the California High School Jazz Band Competition. The competition is scheduled for May 30 at Pacific Grove Junior High School in Pacific Grove.

The ten bands competing will each give 30 minute performances that morning. From there, three bands will be chosen to perform in the finals that night.

While last year's Gunn jazz ensemble was a group dominated by seniors, this year's band is quite the contrary. Containing mostly sophomores and juniors, the band has come together to form a young yet very talented ensemble.

"At the beginning of the year I felt the band was an unexperienced one but also one of strong potential," says jazz band director Rich Prtoese. "I think the band has fulfilled its potential and can still get even better."

The success of the band is truly amazing considering that twelve members, seven of whom were soloists, graduated from the twenty member group of 1980-'81. This loss of talent was cushioned by the sudden upsurge of new soloists from the underclassmen.

"This year, we have had soloists come out of the woodwork to rise to the occasion and perform consistently well throughout the year," stated Prtoese.

While the band is one of great talent, skill is not its only virtue. Hard work and constant extra practice after school have honed and refined the ensemble's lively sounds. Band members have accepted this extra work and believe it has paid off.

"I feel the band has formed into a cohesive unit and so far has exceeded my expectations," said sophomore trombonist David Okner.

The competition favorite is Berkeley High School, winner of the past three competitions and once again the band to beat. However, Prtoese believes Gunn has a good chance to win.

"I am very proud of our band and I feel our chances of winning are as good as any other group's," he states.

Gunn students enjoy New Games Day

By LISE FAVREAU

On Saturday, May 9 on the Gunn football field, close to 300 Gunn students and parents participated in the First Annual Gunn High New Games Day. This fund-raising activity for the senior class was another effort to find alternative activities to drugs and alcohol by Parents Who Care in cooperation with one of the four classes.

Margo Dutton and Pat Theibus, from the Palo Alto Recreation Department, with the help of their equipment, introduced the New Games. The Games were followed by inner tube water polo in the pool and then a dance on the tennis courts.

The main emphasis in New Games is just having fun without creating too much competition. So, within this spirit, the group of 300 students and parents were introduced to several non-competitive games.

A few of these games were played with an "earth ball" (a ball with a bigger diameter than the average sized person). Other games included "people pass" (two close rows of people passed a person over them at arm's length), hug tag (hugging someone else excludes one from getting tagged), and slaughter (slightly related to basketball, but on the knees).

Dutton stated that the day's turnout was very high for a daytime weekend high school activity and she was pleased by the overall success of the day. She added that the Palo Alto Recreation Department has been introducing New Games in other places in Palo Alto and that they can offer their equipment on request.

Earth Ball was one of several activities at New Games Day on Saturday, May 9. The event was sponsored by the senior class and drew approximately 300 participants.

(used with permission)

banner may be used successfully as long as it appears in the upper
third of the paper. But because a floating banner has no fixed position,
it must be worked into the overall design of each front page. Therefore
its column position and height on the page may vary from one issue to
the next.

The Lead Story

There was once a time when the lead story always went in the far
right column. Today it is just as likely to appear in the upper left
or even the center. But wherever the lead starts, given the limited
space offered by the tabloid format, it is best not to cram everything
onto the front page. This means a maximum of three, possibly four
stories can be successfully accommodated.

Tab newspapers are often folded horizontally across the middle
front. This results in a natural division that can be taken advantage
of. If the lead article is run on the top half of the page, one or two
secondary articles will fit nicely on the bottom section. Display
boxes, indexes and important announcements can go into the bottom
corners and work to anchor the page.

Our GRAPEVINE (page 54) shows a variation of this. The line
under the cartoon is right at the fold; below the line is the second
article. The lead story begins in one of the primary optical areas.
The index provides some graphic relief and white space at the bottom
of the page.

What causes one story to be selected as the lead over the others?
Well, in this instance, it was primarily because the lead story was
of local origin, closer to the reader and containing real drama and
conflict. In the long run, the nuclear issue may prove our undoing,
but somehow that seems farther away, less immediate and personal.
In fact, in an effort to personalize the danger of nuclear power, the
author has dramatized a mock evacuation of New York. The closeness,
conflict and human interest make the housing discrimination article
the better lead.

The cluttered front page of this <u>ORACLE</u> is due to overcrowded copy. Lack of visual balance, conflict in the headline typestyles and a boxed calendar poorly placed in the middle of the page add to the confusion. Compare it with the issue on page 58.

(used with permission)

Anchoring the corners.
Graphics on the bottom
of a page are an effec-
tive way of adding eye
appeal to an often visually barren area.

The Basement

Affectionately known as the "basement," the lower half of the front page deserves some focused consideration.   If the paper is folded and tossed upside down on your aunt Martha's coffee table, the bottom portion had best reveal something besides a grey sea of copy.   It's for this reason that in our example the nuclear article headline is deliberately placed below the fold.   Notice, too, that it begins in the area of primary eye travel, falling smack on the diagonal drawn from upper left to lower right.   In addition, the simple index on the bottom of the page acts to lure the eye and helps to identify the paper.

One common technique used to deal with downstairs problems is called "anchoring the corners."   Placing a photograph, graphic or box in each of the lower corners is an easy and effective way to add eye appeal to the basement.   With a tabloid format, however, care must be taken to ensure that the layout doesn't get too cluttered.

The basement copy in our example on page 54 runs in a horizontal

format. Above, the lead story on the left is in what's called a vertical
or "chimney" format. One advantage with horizontal makeup is that
the body of type is visually more compact. Arranged this way, a volume of copy is less likely to repel the reader. For some reason, when
faced with two articles of equal length -- one made up in a single, continuous column and the other in three short, side-by-side columns -- the
reader tends to prefer the horizontal format. The explanation for this
is that horizontal format doesn't look as long and ominous.

Of course, not all stories are important enough to be spread across
the page with a banner headline.   These smaller fellows can be placed
vertically below a horizontally laid out story.   If the lower side of the
horizontal story is not entirely squared off, the headlines won't bump.

At the very bottom of the page go the jumps or continuations. Jumps
are okay, but it's good to keep in mind that a high percentage of readers
never bother to turn the page. To jump a story is annoying and often
just enough of a pain that the story is never finished. What's more, if
a reader does turn the page, what's to bring him back to the front once
again? Therefore, the moral is simple: if it can be avoided at all, don't
jump a story; try like the devil to fit it all on a single page.

Before finishing the front page overview, one last item deserves a
mention.   The placement of the cartoon under the headline on page 54,
with the copy beginning on the left and reading out of the headline, is
what's known as "canopy" construction. That is, the headline canopies
the picture or graphic. Canopy construction is a very effective way of
handling headlines, copy and pictures on a front page. Another common
progression is from picture to caption to headline to copy. Either way,
the idea is to not let the picture get between the headline and the copy.

Breathing Room

As we pointed out before, white space is what gives a page breathing
room and fresh air. Perhaps the single biggest mistake made on community newspapers is the mad attempt to cram everything possible onto
a page until not a single open space remains. The solution to this is to
relax. Then apply the formula on page 64.

Lack of "breathing room" is what mars the copy in this <u>CAMPANILE</u>, another student newspaper. All the elements of good graphic appeal are present here, but they need to be re-arranged. The front page could be improved easily by lowering the floating banner to mid-page and organizing the copy in a format similar to that of the <u>ORACLE</u> on page 58.

The Campanile

Vol. LIV   Palo Alto High School, March 6, 1981   No. 11

Students Oppose Intervention

BY TINA SCHLER

SIGNS SUCH AS this decorated the Paly campus during El Salvador Week. The week was devoted to El Salvador demonstrations and presentations.   Photo by Dan Sakols

Reagan Cutbacks Dent District Funds

By JIM NEWTON

Faculty Investigates Heating

BY PAUL CHAMBERLAIN

IN A LUNCHTIME senior prank last Friday six unidentified seniors carted a twenty foot long joint through the campus. The group paraded in front of the wall and through the library to the applause and cheers of the onlookers.

(used with permission)

Spacing Formula --

Leave 3/16 of an inch:
- (a)   Under the banner
- (b)   Above pictures
- (c)   Below captions
- (d)   Above and below boxes
- (e)   At the end of a story

Leave 1/8 of an inch:
- (a)   Between pictures and captions
- (b)   Between headlines and copy
- (c)   Between headlines and by-lines
- (d)   Above ads

Contrast and Balance

Besides white space, there is a second crucial guiding principle
which beginners should pay attention to. This is the concept of contrast.   Contrast in headlines is obtained by alternating full, heavy
heads with a set of the same typeface or family in italics.   The example from the GRAPEVINE on page 54 demonstrates such contrast.
Another way of doing the same thing is to vary the solid upper case
headlines in one bank or row with all lower or upper-lower case headlines in another.   In a somewhat similar fashion, visual contrast is
accomplished in the copy body itself by the insertion of boxes, photos
and cutlines of different width and depth.

Of course it's important that white space and other visual contrasts
be worked together until a visual harmony and balance is achieved on
a page. Yet when discussing visual harmony, it's necessary not to confuse it with absolute symmetrical balance, although the two are inter-
related. In a well laid out page, things are almost always tipped or
weighted in one direction or another. In fact, a perfectly symmetrical
newspaper page would appear very odd to the eye indeed.

One way to get an idea of the concept of balance in page layout is to consider the optical center of a page a sort of pivot or fulcrum. Then, string the display items -- headlines, boxes, pictures, cartoons -- on it like a flat mobile. Here, as with a mobile, some imbalance is great, providing motion and life to the layout.   Too much imbalance, however, will cause the whole affair to come crashing down around our ears. When weighing display items, a number of things should be kept in mind:

(a)   A photo or graphic on the top half of the page weighs more than an identical one on the bottom half.

(b)   Display items on the right side of a page slightly outweigh those on the left.

(c)   Darker-toned or color items are heavier than light display items.

(d)   Photos that are elongated either horizontally or vertically weigh more than square ones which have the same area.

The GRAPEVINE on page 54 is nowhere near a perfect symmetrical balance. Yet it is an example of harmonious makeup.   To point out the difference: imagine if in our example a second large cartoon of equal size and weight were installed in the lower left quadrant of the front page.   The absurdity and unattractiveness of this are immediately apparent. In fact, about the only time such an exact balance might prove useful would be to highlight parallels or to give equal play to two sides of an issue, as, for example, in an election campaign.

Thinking about all of this, it may dawn on you that harmonious and directed imbalance can give a motion or dynamic quality to a page. Indeed, this is the case with our GRAPEVINE front page. Here we demonstrated how the layout was used in a roundabout

way to propel the eye from the upper left-hand corner to the lower
right. This particular format is an old newspaper formula known
as "turn column" makeup. Turn column goes back to the days when
newspapers were double folded and the "turned" column was displayed
on open racks. Today, it is still a useful device as it conforms to
the natural reading patterns and slides the eye into stories that are
likely to be overlooked otherwise. Turn column can be very useful
on inner pages also. Here pyramiding the ads in a stepdown arrangement can be used not only to guide the eye but also to avoid lumping
all the ads in a rectangular mass on the bottom of the page.

Inside Pages
    Inside page makeup is similar to front-page makeup. Inside pages,
though, must contend with an important added factor -- advertising.
Construction of these pages becomes a joint effort between the

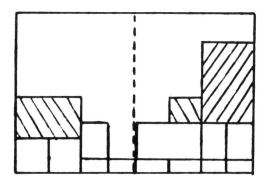

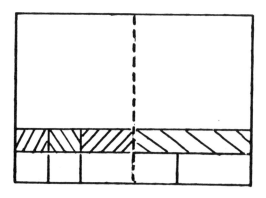

Two types of advertising makeup.
The diagrams illustrate pyramid
style ad makeup above, versus
a horizontal style below.   Horizontal style makeup is probably
easier to deal with, providing all
ads are of a uniform size. Pyramiding the ads, however, is an
effective way of dealing with a
large volume of advertising when
the size and shape is not uniform.

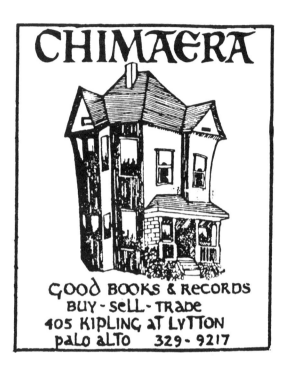

GOOD BOOKS & RECORDS
BUY - SELL - TRADE
405 KIPLING aT LYTTON
PaLo aLTo   329 - 9217

news team and the advertising crew. Ads are usually placed on the page first, then the news copy. Yet this does not necessarily mean that the advertising is most important. Unless you're distributing an advertising sheet, the news copy of the paper is what gets top billing.

This makes guidelines to ad placement a straightforward proposition. News copy goes in the primary optical areas; the ads go elsewhere, as the diagrams on the previous page

Three display ads showing good use of white space and eye-catching graphics. Note how two of them advertise a specific item price on what they sell. Including the price is very important if the ad is to sell successfully. Customers tend to infer an omitted price is a high one.

Hammocks
$43 & $44

558 Santa Cruz Ave., Menlo Park / 323-0313

COPIES
3-1/2¢
each overnight
No minimum

kinko's   299 California Ave
Palo Alto
328-3381

illustrate. It's also important to try to keep the top half of a page
free for copy. But if the ads do pile so high as to approach the top
of the page, then the rule is to construct a pyramid into the copy
area on the right-hand page only, where it falls into the fallow corner at the top right.   On left-hand pages, ads shouldn't violate the
upper corner, which should always be reserved for copy.

It's good to keep in mind that it's the newscopy, not the advertising,
that makes your paper a good one. Ads are important because they
pay the rent, but a newspaper shouldn't get its priorities confused.
If the volume of advertising is so great that the copy is consistently
being squeezed off the page -- congratulations, you're on your way
to fulfilling the American dream. Try increasing the number of pages
in the next issue or go back and see if the ads can't be laid out in a
more compact fashion. Of course this may not be your problem at all.
If advertising volume is small and the ads are relatively of the same
proportion, then the easiest solution is to place them in a horizontal
makeup at the bottom of the page.

When dealing with advertising, one problem that crops up time
and again is that of preferred position. Some advertisers insist on
the back page, others want the middle of page three.   The best way
to handle this headache is to refuse to sell ads by the page -- or if
you do, to charge them dearly for the option.   Having to place ads
on certain pages can wreak havoc with the news. It's almost always
a lot more trouble than it's worth.   A good ad will draw attention
placed almost anywhere in the paper. Incidentally, another common
jealousy among advertisers is the insistence that their display be
separated from the competition. This means no two stereo shop ads
are on the same page or even facing pages, for that matter. This
sounds like a lot of foolishness and it may well be, but it's also something to be wary of.

What Makes a Good Ad?

What makes a good ad? Studies show ads which display the merchandise in an uncluttered manner, contain a price, have brief and

to-the-point copy, and are well arranged artistically and typograph- ically are the ones that sell. The examples on page 67 fit this description.

Once the ad pattern is established, there are a few other princi- ples which apply to inside page makeup. Just as the front page has a dominant headline, so should each of the inner pages. If no sin- gle headline dominates the others, then the page tends to take on a cluttered and uninviting look. The dominant headline should be a good deal larger than the others on the page. This means it is at least a column wider and visually higher than the next largest neigh- bor.   Running two or three headlines of the same size on an in- side page causes the reader to grow confused. The readership expects you to tell them which of the stories is most important.

On inner pages, just as on the front page, the same optical rules hold true.   This means most pages need an attention grabber in a primary optical area. Likewise, pages should contain graphics and photos other than advertising, as well as ample white space.   One thing to watch out for on inner pages is locating illustrations adja- cent to ad photos or graphics. A reader can often mistake the copy illustration for advertising and pass over it.

Worknotes

It's worthwhile looking over some of the examples in this chapter for flaws in makeup. The ORACLE on page 58 is certainly well com- posed by any standards, but can you spot its single defect? It's the top most headline running across the photo on the right. This layout would be improved somewhat if the headline ran in two decks to the left of the photo and not above it. Notice, though, how the ORACLE succeeds in getting all the story copy on the page without having to resort to continuations, something the GRAPEVINE and CAMPANILE never manage to do. This is a good practice as many readers will never bother to finish the story otherwise.

Studying the second ORACLE on page 60 is also instructive. The overcrowded copy is the major problem, but there are others. One

of them is the badly composed headline, "Lot Safened." What does
this headline say, if anything, to the reader? Other difficulties
include the fancy border around the photo and article on the right
which adds clutter to an already overcrowded page and the lack of
by-lines on the majority of articles. By-lines are important to
student and other volunteer journalists. On a volunteer paper,
by-lines serve as an incentive to the author. For some writers,
their unpaid work offers them their only chance to see their names
in print. By-lines are important, too, to curious readers who
want to know who wrote the stories.

Inside Pages
One of the most difficult pages to lay out inside a newspaper is
the editorial and opinions page. Very often this is the second page
of a small newspaper. Our examples on pages 71 and 72 show two
such pages from student newspapers. Here, the first editorial
page from the <u>CAMPANILE</u> wins hands down. Both examples contain significant amounts of copy, but observe how the first breaks
it up using cartoons, graphics and headlines in a harmonious manner that would do any newspaper proud. The <u>ORACLE</u> could have
improved its page by cutting copy, enlarging the tiny graphics and
taking the boxes from around the headlines. The <u>CAMPANILE</u>
demonstrates what metropolitan papers learned long ago: a funny,
prominently displayed cartoon does wonders to enliven an editorial
page.

While we're on the subject of inner pages, two other dangers to
mention are known affectionately as "naked columns" and "tombstoning."
Naked columns result when no picture or headline introduces copy
at the top of a page. Usually this occurs on continuations. A small
headline is the remedy. Tombstoning describes a situation where
headlines run so close as to jam and bump each other like tombstones.
The solution here is to simply rearrange the page layout.

2 January 30, 1981

OPINION
The Campanile

Council Deserves Consultation

In two of its recent decisions, the Paly administration has ignored the Student Council despite Jim Shroyer's pledge to use the council as an advisory board.

The issues of library accessibility and attendance policies both clearly affect the entire student body. Accordingly, any administrative action with respect to these areas should require input from the Student Council.

However, Shroyer and the other administrators last week elected, without any such student opinions, to blockade one library entrance and to implement a broad range of new attendance procedures.

While the merits of the decisions may be debated, the disregard of student viewpoints requires attention. If Paly students are to have a role in governing their own environment, their opinions must be sought and respected.

Last year's handling of the CCABC schedule conflict testified to the success made possible by allowing the student body this degree of self determination. Before deciding on what schedule to adopt, the administration polled students for their ideas and suggestions. Students convincingly supported the CCABC plan, and the schedule has worked smoothly ever since.

Shroyer acknowledges the importance of student perspectives, but his recent actions have not reflected this concern.

The newly elected Student Council and the new administration should be encouraged to meet weekly to trade suggestions for school improvement. These meetings would benefit both parties by allowing the administrators a chance to hear fresh ideas from the students and by letting the students have more of a say in their school's policies.

WELL, THAT'S MY NEW PROPOSAL.... ANY COMMENTS?.....

BIG JIM

STUDENT COUNCIL

WISE 81

LETTERS TO THE ED

We, members of the Alternative Program wish to voice our opinion about the article we wrote for the Campanile issue of December 19. The article's theme was maintained, however, the article's authors were not given credit for their efforts. The article was a guest column, and we feel that guest writers deserve as much acknowledgement for articles as do members of your staff. We put

in a lot of time, work, and energy into perfecting the article and would like the readers to know just who was describing the Alternative Program. We support the idea of having a guest column, but feel the guest contributors should be identified and acknowledged for their hard work.
Karen Brewster, Karen Davidson, Mike Kass, Colleen Powers, Jennifer Trossman, and Lisa Whisnant

NO RESPECT
by JEFF ELDER

As the second semester of my senior year begins, I think I'm finally discovering that education is worthwhile, after all.

I've thought for the last few years that the classrooms, teachers, even the school, were very funny. There are so many funny things in school! Can you imagine one of the math portables exploding during brunch? The topics are funny. In European History you can make it with Plato; in mythology there's Stu, the god of chili; in chemistry the white mice are dying, no one's yet discovered that the laboratories are giving them cancer. The places are funny. In the lecture centers you're flying in a jet; in the library you're holding mass in church; in the math portables you're sitting around in a mobile home; in the old building you're checking into the Hotel California. The teaching methods are funny. New math explains why, not just how, then why math? In English, when you read Shakespeare you translate every line and then interpret every word, yes, his works have survived well, especially with preservatives. Funniest of all is the whole idea. Thousands of bikes,

looking like metallic animals wait for thousands of backpacked riders. Hundreds of people sit at rallies and eat. Why not skip the entertainment, and just have everyone stand up and tell what they're eating?

Yes, school and education are very funny. But, as I said, I've discovered that they are worthwhile. It's important to me to understand what people are talking about and to know what I'm talking about (we can't lie all the time). How have I discovered that they are worthwhile? Well, in wondering why I am staying at school for the second semester of my senior year, rather than leaving Paly early, like some friends of mine, I discovered that education is like new math, it can't answer the question why. It's just there, something to gain and understand, something basic in principle but complex, and funny, in method. Like technology, it makes life better, more advanced. (Technology is very funny, too. Imagine scientists making huge paper towels to soak up spilled radiation and oil.) Some education is like butter on the bread of life. Japanese culture and history is a pure pleasure to study. Some is

very practical. My dad, "Jeff, you really should learn chemistry." Me, "Sorry, dad, that's too funny (people in white coats unable to make a spark with a striker so that they can look at different color gases)."

The worst reason for education is this: It opens doors all over the world. The only reasons that those doors are there is because some educated carpenter got bored and decided to build them.

The best reason for education is this: It's better than working. But there are other good ones, it allows you to meet different types of people (girls and boys), it allows you to know yourself by posing personal questions, it allows you the chance to dream (some of the best dreams that I've ever experienced have been in class), and finally, it develops the imagination.

Imagination is very important in the universe, and since education contributes to it, education is very good.

Without an educationally trained imagination where would Kurt Vonnegut Jr., Ronald Reagan, especially Nancy Reagan, and B. Kliban be today? I don't know, but I can imagine.

The Campanile

Editor-in-Chief
Tim Newton

Managing Editor
Paul Chamberlain

Associate Editor
Jeff Elder

News Editor
Judson Lobdell

Editorials Editor
Forrest Maltzman

Features Editor
Andrew Baum

Sports Editors
Bill McIntyre
Greg Lush

Reviews Editor
Jeff Butler

Ad Managers
Jerry Scher
Mark Diamond

Photographers
Dan Sakols
Ron Fried

Advisor
Mr. Robert Neff

Artists
Todd Foreman
Kirk Wise

Reporters
Andy Baum, Tina Bechler, Anne DeLong, Sheila Henry, Laban Hinton, Leslie Jonath, Marcy Lee, Kevin Petersen, Dede Turnbull, Lesley Yarborough

ALRIGHT CLASS TODAY WE WILL GO OVER OUR 2,000 VOCABULARY WORDS AND....

HA HA HA HA... HA HA

WEASELS

10/11

IT'S A SENIOR!! HA! HA!

I THINK WE'VE JUST SEEN THE FIRST SIGNS OF SENIORITIS!

OH NO IT'S STARTED, YOU FILTHY HEATHEN!!!

OH NO COME BACK HERE

BY TODD FOREMAN

(used with permission)

An excellently composed editorial page. This student newspaper uses cartoons, graphics and headlines to full advantage.

SEPTEMBER 26, 1980 THE ORACLE PAGE 2

A new start for the Oracle

The ORACLE has undergone many changes this year, including the editorial staff, which you can see below, policy alterations, and plans to produce a paper every two weeks (except for the special edition), which comes to eighteen papers for the whole year as opposed to eleven last year. All these are substantial changes, but the single largest difference this year has been the loss of Mrs. Carol Jones, teacher and advisor for The ORACLE and the journalism classes for the past three years, who suddenly died of a massive heart attack two days before school began.

I really respected Mrs. Jones for the way she respected journalism. Also for the manner in which she went about trying to give her students the best knowledge and experience which work in the classroom and on The ORACLE. She always wished for The ORACLE to be at its finest as far as writing and layout went by the time it was taken to the district office to be printed. We had many a rough time, of course, when Mrs. Jones' interests for the paper conflicted with our (the staff's) wishes, but she was the first to believe in compromise. To her, putting out The ORACLE was a job of team work. Mrs. Jones took an interest in every member of the staff, from the editors on down to the beginning journalism student.

Despite this unfortunate loss of Mrs. Jones, The ORACLE, as always, must go on. So we look to the future and the first thing that comes to mind is our new advisor-teacher for journalism, Tom Harbeck, a graduate student at Stanford. Mr. Harbeck, though havpng limited experience in journalism, has a fine

EDITORIAL

background in English after majoring in that subject at Trinity College in Hartford, Connecticut. The inexperience will not be much of a problem, seeing as how The ORACLE is a "student-run newspaper," and Mr. Harbeck will have plenty of time to observe the editing and production procedures first-hand during the first few issues. Mr. Harbeck at the same time has no plans to just watch The ORACLE be produced, but will spend plenty of time advising while at the same time teaching the beginning class the basics of journalism, which he himself is just now starting to absorb.

Indeed, Mr. Harbeck has hit The ORACLE in its own "hard times." With the "Jones Era" having come to a halt, The ORACLE has the extra burden this year of bearing a bedget which is 400 in the hole. With money coming only from subscriptions and ads in The ORACLE's past and a steep printing bill returning itself to take from the paper's coffers every issue, a balanced budget has been as rare with The ORACLE as with the United States government. This year, though, our Gunn newspaper has been helped out by the Student Executive Council. We will be selling soft drinks at tonight's dance and possibly the rest. This revenue could be the savior of our reddened budget. This year will definitely be a learning experience for Mr. Harbeck.

So, though we have lost a great figure in Gunn journalism, Carol Jones, and have inherited a wealth of economic problems, we have also gained a new advisor in Tom Harbeck and, hopefully, a new look for The ORACLE.

Andres Fajardo
Editor-in-Chief

The ORACLE, an official publication of the Associated Students of Gunn High School, Palo Alto, California, is published bi-monthly by the Journalism Classes.

Editor-in-Chief . . . . Andres Fajardo
Managing Editor . . . . Jon Streifer
Associate Editor . . . . Marsh McCall
Production Editor . . . . Nancy Whitaker
Sports Editor . . . . Mark Weiss
Photography Editors . . . . Brad Elman, Steve Presnell
Business Manager . . . . Sara MacPherson
Circulation Manager . . . . Ann Vandenberg
Production Manager . . . . Vivian Chin

Staff:
Lisa Baker, Claire Barry, Robin Brann, Dave Carnoy, Jonathon Carnoy, Connie Cervantes, Charlie Cosovich, Lisa Delong, Lise Farreau, Rodrigo Flores, Dorian Fondahl, Robert Goodwin, Eric Hager, Murphy Halliburton, Rhonda Harris, Jon Kaplan, Aaron Kaufmann, Steve McGrouther, Liz Nelson, Greg Nerland, Robert Preston, Pat Siegman, Dan Stryer, Jeff Thornton, Dave Trager, Jeanie Waltuch, Amy Wang, Jean Watt, Kristyn Wiggin.

Seriously, Folks

by Marsh McCall

Latest joke from Wyoming: Why did the monkey fall out of the tree? It was dead. Sorry. That one belongs in Wyoming. And a strange place it is. I was there for a week this summer. I bet you're all asking, "Marsh, what were YOU doing in Wyoming?" Well, mind your own business. Anyway, the people there are really weird. They say "Get along there," when they mean "hurry up" and they say "Hello" when they mean "Gosh" and they say, "What did you have for breakfast?" when they mean "What did you have for breakfast?" It was nice riding horseback in the Teton mountains but I felt sorry for the grooms. Keep horses in a crowded stable for an hour and the work really starts piling up. If you know what I mean.

That's about it for my summer. Except for my job at Roundtable Pizza. It's a pretty good job but I'm now so sick of pizza that whenever someone mentions the word I begin sweating and have to change my pants.

Let's get serious for a moment though. Several people told me last year that I am not funny. My mother tells me this is not so but I am still deeply hurt. However, I am not going to stand here and receive insults from inferiors. To prove that I am funny I have made a list of people I am more humorous than. I have put a star by the names of people I am McCall funnier than:

Tarzan
Any of Tarzan's apes
Anyone else Tarzan knows, including Jane
Anyone Jane knows
*Gerald Ford
Adolf Hitler
Amy Carter
Satan
*small rodents
inanimate objects, such as rocks or pencil sharpeners
nuclear warheads
*Aaron Kaufmann
(Not necessarily in this order)

The Rabelaisian

by David Trager

I'm a senior. One can easily distinguish seniors during the first semester by our panic-stricken expressions, glazed eyes and trembling fingers. The source of this unnerving affliction? Just mention the word "application" or "test registration form" and you may reduce a self-respecting upperclassman to quivering jelly or a hysterically giggling loon.

Having registered for the PSAT, the SAT, several AP tests and numerous Achievements, we seniors have become masters of the Educational Testing Service application forms. Only us veterans know what lurks behind those seemingly innocuous questions:

1. Name... elementary. We seniors do not suffer from identity crises. After all, if you spell your name correctly the ETS will automatically give you a 200. I chcked my birth certificate to make sure.
2. Birthdate... the ETS obviously wants to make sure that they have the right to confiscate the liquor you bring to settle pre-test jitters. *Sigh*.
3. Sex... I, for one, think that's rather private. "F" obviously stands for "frequently" but "M"? I'm still figuring that one out. The ETS leaves you no pride.
4. Mailing Address & Phone Number... note that they ask you for both. This is to insure that you get the bad news one way or another.

From there on the questions take on the qualities of a cross-examination. The ETS wants to know everything... and I mean EVERYTHING about you. They are worse than the IRS and very likely related. For example, they are interested in one's financial situation and the number of people dependent upon their families for support. If you cheated on your income tax forms, the ETS will ferret you out and turn you over to cousin IRS. Then they'll probably flunk you on the SAT too, regardless of whether you spelled your name correctly.

The ETS lets you know that there is no escape. Just look at the number of testing center codes. The ETS is everywhere! They obviously subscribe to the Surround and Infiltrate tactic. If you see seniors furtively looking over their shoulders, it's not always because of crib-notes. It's because we never really know where another testing center will appear. From the deepest jungles of Peru to the icy vastness of Iceland, from the dust bowls of Oklahoma to the shores of Honolulu....this land is YOUR land ETS.

Seniors also suffer side effects from the problems mercilessly inflicted by the ETS. I, for instance, have Blipitis. This is a particularly unsettling condition that strikes those subjected to Number Two Pencil Syndrome. Please blacken the ovals, they say. Do not press too hard, they request. Do not color too lightly, they demand. Are you using a number two pencil? they ask sweetly after you've finally finished your two hundredth blip using a hard lead pencil. I now dream about those blips.

You see, the ETS is the source of a notorious plot to become... shudder... Big Brother. They want to see a number two pencil in every hot little hand. Yes, we the class of '81 have it tough, but I really feel for the freshmen... alias the class of 1984. Big Brother'll be watching you...

The Nose Knows

By AARON KAUFMANN

"This fall you face a very important decision which will have a great impact on the rest of your life." This frightening line began in a letter from St. Joe's North East South Dakota Mining College. Almost all of the college information brochures open in this fashion. Out of my 32 college packets (junk mail), 10 of the letters opened with the exact, word for word line as S.J.N.E.-S.D.M.C. did above. I cannot wait until these schools get in trouble for violation of the copyright laws.

There are other points in common in these sales packets. Virtually all of the schools claim to be one of the top institutions in the country. (I'm sure glad I get letters from top colleges, like S.J.N.E.S.D.-M.C., instead of scummy Ivy league schools.)

These colleges also claim to harbor a fantastic campus life to be located near a major cultural metropolis. S.J.N.E.-S.D.M.C. claims these attributes and backs them up with facts. "The culturally refined city of Armspitnik, South Dakota is within an hour's drive of our beautiful campus. The city plays host annually to the circus and the county fair. Armspitnik is also home of the semi-finals of the National Buffalo Chip Throwing Contest," writes the Dean of S.J.N.E.-S.D.M.C.

One can figure out a college's size and type of educational program by the words used in their pamphlets. The small liberal arts colleges use words and phrases such as 'unique, communication, personal growth, building of relationships' and 'sense of community.' The larger schools boast about what there great size can provide the student with, 'diversity, side range of choice, a 1 million volume library' and 'a great defensive line for the football team.'

Due to all these similarities between the pamphlets distributed by each college, it is hard to decide the right college to apply to. To solve this problem my friend has developed a system of choosing colleges to apply to. He informs me, "the first step is to study the pictures in the pamphlets. If these pictures include nice scenery of the female persuation, one finds more information on the college. One should look up the school's location, ratio of males to females and the campus' rules on student behavior. Then, if the school still looks interesting, one should pay a visit to its campus. During one's visit, one should check out the housing and how close it is to the beach or other recreation. One should also attend a party, in order to experience the campus atmosphere."

Joke for people with calculators on the belts and who read chemistry text books for fun: Hear the one about the sulfate ion that was arrested for molecular bondage?
(Thank you Jon Kaplan for that witty pun. If you would like to send dirty letters to Jon write to "Jon's John of Jokes, P.O. Box 245, Palo Alto, Calif.")
Off the Wire: Scientists have predicted a major air pollution problem in the Los Altos Hills area, due to the increase in diesel automobiles on the roads. The problem became noticeable about the time the Mercedes Benz Turbodiesel came off the assembly line.
Grafitti of the Week: Clones for Abortion! (This was written in big letters on an overpass in, where else, but San Francisco.)
Bumper Sticker of the Week: Nuke the Gay Iranian Whales. (That just about offends everyone, so I will stop now. Konnichiwa Reader san....)

(used with permission)

"Cramped" describes this editorial page. Greatly enlarged graphics, more white space and less copy would improve this layout.

VI
Preparation for Layout

Layout and pasteup are the terms used to describe the mechanics
of preparing photo-ready copy for offset printing. This has to do with
how the various elements of a page -- the headlines, articles, cartoons, ads and halftoned photos -- are assembled and pasted down in
preparation for printing. Large sheets of ruled paper, known as flats,
are used and the elements to be printed are laid down and attached
with wax or rubber cement to these flats. When the layout is complete,
the flats are carted off to the printer and photographed with a special
camera. Hence the term "camera-ready" copy.

Your obligations are ended once the camera-ready flats are in the
printer's hands. What the printer does then is photographically transfer the image off the flats onto a very thin sheet of metal called a
plate. As described in chapter one, the plate is treated so that the
exposed areas attract the ink and the unexposed areas are wetted to
repel it. Then the plate is wrapped around a cylinder on which the
blank paper turns, transferring the image from the plate to the paper
and giving the process its name, photo offset. Just about anything
that can be photographed can be printed using this method. Strike-
on type, copy produced by a typewriter with a carbon ribbon, is
ideal. Most important, the cumbersome, expensive and complicated
equipment necessary to produce hot type is completely eliminated.
All this sounds simple enough, and indeed, the basics of pasteup and
layout are. But, like so many other things in life from lovemaking
to cooking, people can learn the rudiments on a single afternoon,
only to spend the rest of their lives improving and perfecting variations on the initial theme.

Full-scale dummy.   From a thumb-nail sketch, the full-scale dummy is drawn up. The dummy does not have to be exact in every detail, but it is the blueprint from which the final page is drawn up.   Notice how the type style here duplicates the final choice on page 54.   The headline composition, however, only approximates the end product.

In the discussion of format, it was shown how newspaper layout is primarily functional. That is, its major purpose is to make the news copy inviting and easy to read. Front pages especially are designed to capture the eye as well as the imagination from a considerable distance. But even if the front page is the most important, the layout on all pages should attract and make the copy appealing.

When planning the layout, it's good to try and conceptualize the paper or leaflet as an organic whole: balanced, attractive to the eye, and easy to read and understand. A work of art is more than paint haphazardly smeared across a canvas. Similarly, a well laid out newspaper, leaflet or newsletter has its own deliberate order, visual tensions and internal structure.

It's important to stress that a painfully researched and otherwise well-written article may never secure the audience it deserves just because it's badly laid out or suffers from a poorly composed or misleading headline. So too, sloppy, careless page design automatically reflects on the written content, implicitly conveying the message that the journalism is likewise arrived at in a jumbled, illogical, inaccurate fashion. With this in mind, it therefore follows that anything which confuses or distracts from the copy readability should be avoided.

So it becomes necessary to follow a few elementary rules in order to arrive at a successful layout. Most of them are simple applications of the techniques we discussed when examining over-all format.

-- Always take care that headlines and illustrations are well chosen and separated by lots of breathing room from copy.
-- White space should be generously used to insulate various elements from each other and to keep heads from bumping.
-- Although dominant elements are needed, don't overdo it. Make sure one dominant element, such as a powerful illustration or photo, doesn't absorb all the reader's attention and dilute the total impact. Balance is the key.
-- If the eye is left searching and a person has to perform mental acrobatics to determine where to start reading, the layout has failed in its primary purpose.

In the end, simplicity is the key to good layout. Like a Zen rock garden which captures the eye and stimulates the imagination in its unobtrusive order and neatness, a good layout also has an almost invisible focus and center.

From Draft to Front Page

In order to understand how all this works, let's take a look at the process involved from edited draft to final publication in the front page article about housing discrimination in the GRAPEVINE. The first step in that process is editing and typesetting the original copy.

Double spaced and with corrections penciled in, the edited draft is okayed for typesetting. Actually the type isn't "set" at all. What happens in the case of the GRAPEVINE is that the copy is retyped to

First step in news production, preparing the original copy. Here is the original draft of the front page housing article. The circled 850 at the top is a word count necessary to estimate the overall space allocations for copy in the newspaper.

Sue Luttner
March 20, 1976

WHAT COLOR ARE THE TAN APARTMENTS

Eight years after the Civil Rights Act of 1968 outlawed racial discrimination in housing, two Palo Alto apartment managers are charging that they have been fired because they did not discriminate.

Now Pamela and Jerry Donnelly are taking it to court in an effort to ~~regain their jobs~~ and put an end to what they consider discrimination by the Youritan Construction Company. The "Tan" apartments include approximately 1,000 units in several complexes scattered about Palo Alto. The Donnellys managed the Tan Village complex, bordering Amarillo ~~and~~ ~~Co.?~~ Ave. in south Palo Alto from July, 1975 until this February.

In an affidavit regarding her and her husband's employment by Tan, Pamela said, "On numerous occasions we were expected to tell minorities there were not vacancies that really existed, direct them to certain sections of apartments, apply different standards of income evaluation, treat them differently than whites when rent payments were late, delay needed apartment repairs and improvements when minority tenants requested them."

James Wolpman, a lawyer for the Donnellys, called this behavior "second level discrimination," which he said is harder to prove than open hostility.

Tan's attorney Neil Falconer told the GRAPEVINE, "Our client does not discriminate." He also said that Tan had "good" and sufficient" reasons for discharging the Donnellys.

Pamela and Jerry started working for Tan last summer. At the

column specifications on an IBM Executive typewriter. Setting the margins at 3 5/16 inches and using a non-photoreproducing blue pencil line as a right margin guide, the typist simply produces a column of finished copy which will later be corrected and pasted to a flat.

There are a number of good reasons for using the IBM Executive typewriter. Most important is the cost. Professional typesetting is expensive and could easily run over $150 an issue for a 16-page newspaper. An IBM Executive rents for about $20 a week or $40 a month. A good reconditioned Executive sells for between $350 and $450. The GRAPEVINE owns one Executive outright and rents a second identical machine for the one week each month it produces the paper. This is the way the newspaper's typesetting costs are kept under $25 an issue.

Another advantage to this particular machine is the variable unit spacing. Thus an m receives three times the amount of space afforded to an i or an l. The effect upon the eye is that the copy has been professionally typeset on some fancy machine. In fact, if the copy is slightly reduced, about the only way it can be distinguished from set copy is the uneven or ragged right margin. The ragged right seems a small price to pay compared with the budget cost of typesetting any other way. An added benefit of the Executive is that its special carbon ribbon, which gets used only once and does not recycle, produces the clean, dark image necessary for good photo reproduction.

So, using an IBM Executive, the copy gets retyped in the correct format on good quality 8 1/2" x 14" legal-size paper. Some papers choose at this point to use a special hard, slick paper. Although the quality of reproduction of this special paper is better than good bond, it has its drawbacks. One is the high cost. Another is the fact that the paper is so hard and glossy that it does not absorb the ink, and, if handled carelessly, the copy smears. This necessitates using a spray can of fixer, adding more expense. For all this, the benefits seem small.

Once the copy is typeset, it is cut out and pasted to the flat. A flat is just a large sheet of heavy paper, usually measuring 17 1/2" x 23",

The faint blue pencil line guides the typist on the right margin in the typeset copy. When an error is made, the whole line is retyped next to the one it will replace. Notice that the fifth paragraph is completely crossed out and has been retyped. When the copy is ready to be pasted, this paragraph will be snipped out and the column rejoined.

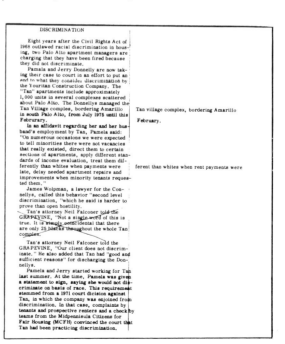

with column grids printed on the back. The column grids usually
come in either a five-column or six-column format. The flats themselves are obtained at the printshop.

The flats are taped down on the glass top of a light table (page 84),
using masking tape on each corner. The light projecting up from under
the frosted glass top of the table reveals the grid pattern and allows the
copy, captions and headlines to be accurately spaced and arranged. The
GRAPEVINE uses a six-column flat, doubling up every two columns on
the flat to arrive at a three-column format.

Pasteup

There are two methods used to affix copy to the flats. One involves
the use of rubber cement, the other, hot wax. Rubber cement is cheap
and a straightforward layout agent. Copy is affixed simply by coating
the back of the text with cement and laying it on the flat. As it takes a
few minutes for the cement to dry, the copy can be slid around and adjusted in place. Later, if it needs to be pulled up after drying, rubber
cement thinner can be used. A liquid solvent, the thinner is squirted
under a corner of the copy,which comes loose easily by alternately peel-
ing and applying more solvent. The thinner dries rapidly and will not
damage copy or smear ink.

One drawback to rubber cement is that it tends to get all over everything. You will find it between your fingers, in your beard, and all
over the coffee pot. There is a little device called a rubber cement
pick-up which will aid much in combating these drawbacks. This inexpensive block of gum-rubber-like substance is invaluable in keeping copy
clean. But even so, constant vigilance is necessary when using rubber
cement to keep the stuff from getting over everything.

Hot wax, the other method used to paste things down, has a lot of
advantages. The only real drawback is locating or purchasing a waxing machine. A secondhand one might be had for less than $100, if you
are lucky. Then there's always the possibility of borrowing one from
a school or university during the days of actual production. Otherwise

plan on investing a couple of hundred bucks. The big advantage to
wax is that it doesn't attract dirt, and copy can be easily removed
without resorting to solvent.   Rewaxing simply requires another
run through the machine. About the only thing a waxer won't handle
is very small bits of copy, which it has a habit of dumping into
the molten wax. Resorting to rubber cement or a spray fixative
in a pinch can solve this problem. All around, wax is a better,
neater approach to pasteup. In fact, about the only real drawback
is the investment in equipment.

Headlines

    To produce headlines, there are again two options.   The first
is to use rub-off type or transfer lettering.   Available in most art
supply stores, transfer lettering has many advantages. Letraset,
Normatype and Format are a few of the trademarks which produce more styles and sizes than any newspaper could ever use.

    Transfer lettering is printed on clear plastic sheets with a
wax adhesive on the back. The lettering is rubbed right onto the
layout by pressing the plastic sheet with a ball-point pen or similar tool and rubbing the lettering off. Alignment is achieved by
drawing a light non-photoreproducing blue pencil line and centering the headline on it. After deciding to use rub-off lettering, the

Transfer Lettering. Dozens
of brands and literally hundreds of type styles of transfer lettering are available
to make rub-off headlines.
Shown is Letraset, one of
the most popular and well-
designed versions.

best way to go is to choose two or three type styles and stick with
those, purchasing sheets of each in 18-, 24-, 36-, and 48-point sizes.
At up to $5 a sheet, this can amount to a considerable investment
in itself.

The second option again involves an equipment purchase. Faster
than rub-off lettering and easy to operate, a strip printer or veri-
type headliner affords speed and flexibility in headline composition
not available to a newspaper using rub-off type. Over the long run
it can save money and a lot of anguish. Using this process, a strip
of photographic film is exposed through a negative image of a letter
to form a headline character by character. Centering and spacing
are determined mechanically and there is no way the characters
can peel off or crack, as often occurs with transfer lettering.

To change type style or size, all that is necessary is to replace
the wheel or negative strip that contains the type master. A dozen
or more headlines of different size or style may be produced in one
run with a headline machine. All around, it's a better solution to
composing headlines -- again, if you can afford it.

Dummies

Before layout can proceed, the overall composition of each page
has to be thought out. The first step in deciding what goes where
is to make a rough, penciled thumbnail sketch of the page. It may
take a half dozen such sketches to work up a balanced dummy. From
there, a full-scale dummy is prepared. This mockup (page 74)
becomes a blueprint for the finished page. Inner pages are dummied
in paired twos. For example, page 2 and 3 are dummied together,
even though they may not be laid out side by side. Type styles, headline size and copy placement are all determined at this point, as well
as placement of photos, illustrations and other graphics. Let's look
at the construction of the front page of our example GRAPEVINE and
follow one of the stories step by step through production from draft
copy to layout and final publication.

Variations of thumbnail sketches. While the copy is being set, thumbnail sketches are drawn to help the layout crew visualize the final layout for the front page. Thumbnails are a very quick way to determine what the pasteup possibilities are. From the thumbnails a full-scale dummy as on page 74 is produced.

Copy Placement

Just before the beginning of pasteup, the GRAPEVINE editorial board meets and considers the recommendations of the various news teams. All the copy is made available for examination. The story's working title, word length and space requirements for graphics and photos are listed on a small blackboard by each subeditor. Once all the copy is placed on the board, a total word count is estimated and priorities are established.

The editors know that on the average about 1,100 words fit comfortably on a GRAPEVINE page. Any more copy than this will not leave ample space for graphics, photos and advertising. For a 16-page newspaper, it's estimated that about 17,600 words is

the maximum that can be accommodated without cramping the layout.
If a total word count reveals too much copy at this point, the board
goes round robin and decides what gets eliminated. Timeliness and
quality of the copy are weighed heavily if cutting is necessary. The
copy itself may be pulled from the stack and examined briefly by all.
But more often than not, each editor understands the copy priorities
and is prepared to recommend cuts and eliminations should they be
required.

Once the overall body of copy is fitted to the number of pages available, the board turns to the front page. Here it debates the merits of
the articles and concludes that the housing discrimination story will
make the best lead.   The nuclear article is slated to accompany it.
Since a photograph of the apartment complex would have been abomi-
nably dull, the staff decides instead to run a modified cartoon snatched
from a GRAPEVINE graphics file. The overall layout of the front page
is discussed in rough terms. A very approximate dummy is sketched
out and this is provided for the layout crew on a sheet of 8 1/2" x 11"
paper. Later a full-scale dummy is prepared.

Copy on inner pages is handled in a similar fashion. In turn, each
story is assigned a page allocation and position on that page. If the
issue is a loose one, two of the back pages can be left relatively open
for overflow, late advertising and announcements. The advertising
coordinator gets into the action at this point and the ads are dealt
out to the inner pages as each page is dummied up on 8 1/2" x 11"
sheets. These quick thumbnail sketches are tacked to a bulletin
board for easy reference once actual pasteup begins.

Typesetting

The first real stage of production commences when the edited and
approved copy is retyped on the IBM Executive typewriter. A good
deal of care is taken when preparing a column to see that the ragged
right margin appears not too ragged. Sometimes whole paragraphs are
retyped because they are especially unsightly or contain more than
three consecutive hyphenated lines. On our final front page, the aver-

age line runs four or five characters one side or the other of the blue line which defines the column width.

To make a blue line at the proper width, the paper is placed in the typewriter and the margin set. Then the column width is measured, at 3 5/16 inches in this case, and a blue dot is lined up beneath one of the small V grooves on the plastic paper guide near the area where the keys strike the paper. Finally, a line is made down the page at the proper width by holding the pencil against the paper and rolling the platen up. The process is repeated for each story going into the paper.

Corrections

If mistakes are made, there are a number of options for correcting them. The first is to use properly thinned liquid paper and white over the offending characters. This works fine for small one- or two-character mistakes or for a single word. But it won't do for larger goofs. Here it becomes necessary to retype a whole line or set of lines. Later, these corrections are pasted on top of the bad copy.

Perhaps an even better method of eliminating the possibility of a correction falling off is to take an x-acto knife or razor blade and cut into the original and tape it from the back. If the typist provides corrections alongside the column, as in the example on page 77, then they become easy to spot and remedy when the copy arrives at the light table. When typing corrections, care should be taken to maintain the original spacing.

When the copy gets to the layout stage, the correction is cut away, leaving plenty of space around it. Then, on a light table, it's superimposed on the bum original. With the two held firmly down, a razor edge is used to cut around the correction and down through the original. The correction then comes to fit exactly the dimensions of the hole cut into the original. With the bad copy removed, the correction is attached to the original using transparent tape applied across the hole in the rear. The nice thing about this approach to corrections is that the patch will line up perfectly with the original copy. As it's flush with the original, it's next to impossible for the correction to work loose or slide out of place.

Pasting It Down

Once a column is typed, it's taken to the light table and the excess paper is carefully cut from both margins of the typed sheet with a pair of scissors. The copy is arranged according to the detailed dummy and cut to fit the column length. Care is taken to leave the allotted space for headlines, and provisional spaces are marked on the flats with non-photo blue pencil where photographs, illustrations, cutlines or other interruptions in the copy will occur. When everything has been fit into place, the copy is run through the waxer or rubber cement is applied and it's carefully stuck down using the horizontal and vertical guidelines illuminated from the back of the flats by the light table. Once every-thing has been fit into place, the columns are double-checked with a straightedge for proper alignment. Anything out of kilter is repasted. Then, the whole page is burnished or rubbed down using a roller and a piece of tracing or tissue paper to ensure that everything will stay put.

Illustrations, halftones (screened photographs) and headlines are handled the same way. They are waxed or cemented to the flat and rubbed down. Again, the ruled lines on the back of the flats ensure proper alignment. If transfer headlines such as Letraset are used, they are first transferred to a sheet of paper and then cut out and fixed to the flats the same as the copy. It would be a mistake to transfer them directly onto the flat. If they break, or if it becomes necessary to shift the layout to accommodate something else on the page, there will be the devil to pay.

Worknotes

A light table is a large illuminated table used for pasteup (page 91). Probably the cheapest way to acquire a light table is to build one yourself. Construction is extremely simple and about everything you need can be gotten secondhand. The table used by the GRAPEVINE is such an example. Measuring approximately 3' x 5' and con-structed out of two old shipping crates, it's illuminated by ten surplus fluorescent fixtures purchased from a local electric shop. The fix-

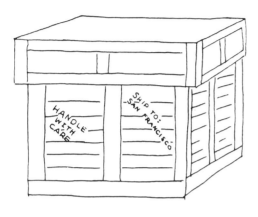

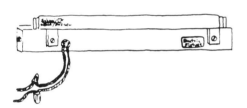

tures are the same type that are used in household kitchens and bathrooms. Each one takes a 15-inch fluorescent bulb. The lights are arranged in even rows along the bottom of the crate, wired together and screwed down tight. A hole in one corner of the crate allows a heavy-duty electric cord to be attached. Frosted plate glass of the correct size and 3/8 of an inch thick was purchased from a local glazier. The glass was cut 1/4 of an inch smaller than the inner dimensions of the crate. Then, a 1" x 2" strip was nailed inside the crate 3/8 of an inch from the top edge. The lights were tested and then the glass was carefully lifted into place in the center of the crate, supported snugly with 1" x 2" strips and flush on all the edges. Thus, with a minimum of expenditure and a few days of hustling and hammering, the GRAPEVINE had a light table big enough that eight pages of newspaper could be pasted down simultaneously.

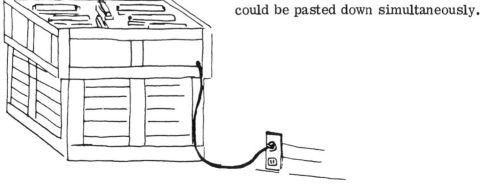

VII
Photography and Halftones

Halftone photography is a special method used to reproduce photographs in printed works such as newspapers, leaflets and newsletters. It involves a dot matrix system which allows the press to print with ink in one color or density, usually black, and make the printed result appear as though it had been reproduced with intermediate shades. From a distance of a few inches, the halftone dots blend together and the eye interprets them in varying shades of grey ranging from almost white to near solid black.

Pick up any newspaper and examine a photograph closely. A pattern of tiny black dots is easily detectable. An offset press or mimeograph can't lay down varying densities of ink. But what they can do is distribute ink onto the paper in areas of different size. If the dots are relatively large and close together, the area will appear almost black. Dots of various intermediate sizes reproduce the midrange of grey tones.

Halftones are made at the print shop by reshooting regular photographs through a special halftone screen. While shooting a halftone, the photo may be enlarged or reduced to the size required by adjusting the process camera. The procedure sounds simple enough, but actually a great deal of skill is required by the camera person to arrive at an acceptable reproduction.

Good halftone reproduction begins with a good photograph. This means one with a good range of tones, or contrast, from the very light to almost black. If a photo is too dark or uniformly grey, it is certain to reproduce poorly. So when choosing a photo for reproduction, look for the shots with the greatest contrast and a wide range of tone

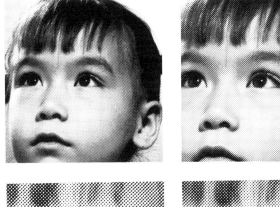
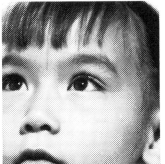
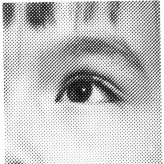
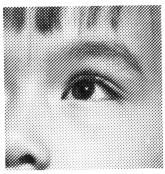

Halftones: Here are progressively enlarged sections of a halftoned photograph, revealing the dot matrix. Hold the page at a distance and observe how the eye acts to blend the dots together on the largest blowup.

(courtesy Eastman Kodak)

values from light to dark. Keep in mind that a halftone screen will put some extra dots in even the whitest and darkest areas. Also remember that photos with an extremely wide range of tones require more work by the camera crew in order to reproduce accurately.

Line Drawings

Line drawings, such as on page 85, seldom create the reproduction problems that photographs often do. Pen and ink illustrations, cartoons and the like do not require halftoning since the lines are all the same density. These reproduce very well on an offset press. Faced with the choice between a muddy photo or an original hand-drawn pen-and-ink rendering, a wise decision would be to run the line drawing. An exception to this is artwork which has washes, such as brush and ink drawings or watercolors. Avoid these like the plague. They require at least two camera shots and then expensive handwork at the printers.

Reproducing halftones from other publications can also be tricky. Sometimes, with luck, it's possible to reproduce the existing screening in the photo. More often, though. it's necessary to rescreen it.

Rescreening becomes complicated as the second set of dots imposed on the first will tend to set up an annoying pattern called a moire. The moire can be reduced by wizardry on the part of the camera person, but some of the finer details will inevitably be lost.

There are easy ways to cut down on halftone expenses. Shot individually, each halftone will cost a few dollars. But if all photos have similar tone values and are to be reproduced at the same percentage, then try ganging them and halftoning all in a single shot. The printed result will give a uniformity to the photos in your publication. The press camera crew will be happier also, because it's a lot easier to shoot one or two ganged shots than a dozen individual ones.

What Makes a Good Photograph?

As we indicated before, contrasty pictures are what make good halftones. This means the blacks are dark, the whites light and a good range of middle-tone greys exist between. Bright light is what makes contrasty pictures. Therefore a photographer should try to shoot with the brightest light possible. Outdoors wait for the sun. Inside, use a flash. Lack of light will result in grey, muddy photographs. In addition, pay careful attention to the background when shooting. A dark subject such as a county administrator in a dull brown suit will tend to get lost in a dimly lit room. A white rabbit will be unrecognizable against a snowdrift. A fancy camera with lots of f-stops and a good light meter will help, but nothing will make up for lack of light.

Getting the Photograph Onto the Page

Getting the photo onto the layout is simple enough. There are two methods used to indicate to the printer which photo goes where. One is to draw a box on the flat in a non-photoreproducing pencil in the exact dimensions where the photo is to go. Inside the box, put an identifier like "3-b, cow." This tells the printer it's the second photo (b) on page 3 and that the picture is of a cow. On the back of the photo to be screened, the same code is lightly penciled.

The other method involves pasting a black piece of paper or rectangle of dark red plastic-like substance called rubylith where the photo is to go. The dark area, called a "knockout," becomes a clear window in the line negative used by the printer to etch the printing plate. A separate halftone negative is made at the print shop. Then this is stripped into the window left in the larger page negative. In either case, it's very important to code the photo original clearly so that the printer will know which halftone to put where.

Blowups and Reductions
    What if a photo is too big or too small for the column space allotted? Then it's necessary to either blow it up or reduce it. Using a proportional wheel (page 97), determine what percentage of the original the half-tone should be. For example, if a photo measures 6" x 10" and it's necessary to fit it into a three-inch column, the reduction would be 50 percent. So along with the "3-b, cow" code on the back of the original would appear a 50 percent reduction notation. Similarly, if a line drawing or cartoon was too small, say 2" x 2", a blowup of 150 percent would be necessary to fit the 3" x 3" result into a three-inch column. Incidentally, if the photo is to go at its original proportions, the notation will be 100 percent to avoid confusion.

Cropping
    If it's not necessary to reproduce all of a photo, then cropping is in order. For example, if it's determined that our 6" x 10" example would go better if an inch were taken off the left side and two from the bottom, two sets of cropping arrows are marked in black along the white margins of the photo. The set on the left, an inch in, is to indicate a crop line there. The set across the bottom indicates a crop two inches up. In this case a reduction of only 75 percent is noted on the back of the original. Thus the picture would be treated as if it measured 4" x 8". Actual cropping would take place on the halftone. The original remains intact and uncut.

Worknotes

Try shooting photographs at a low angle, very near the ground: The
sky makes an excellent background for many subjects.   In addition,
low angle shooting will help eliminate extraneous background clutter
such as buildings, trees and the like.

Shoot close enough to the subject: Take a second to get a sharp focus. Fuzzy pictures make fuzzy halftones.   Try to make the subject
fill the frame as much as possible.   Use a telephoto lens if necessary.
A great deal of enlarging in the darkroom will result in loss of focus
and contrast.

Read up on photography: A good place to start is with some of the
Kodak manuals available at photo supply stores. Manual Q-3, Halftone Methods for the Graphic Arts, is especially helpful.

Warning!   Color photographs do not reproduce like their black and
white cousins. All those nice color tones are likely to be reduced
to mud when translated back to black and white by the halftone process.   Take this on faith and keep only black and white film in your
camera when taking photos for reproduction purposes.

VIII
Tools

The office requirements to publish even something as extensive as a small newspaper are quite modest. For a newspaper all that you need are a half dozen mechanical typewriters, a phone, two or three old desks with lots of drawers, some shelves, a filing cabinet or two. For a newsletter or something less ambitious, obviously the requirements are even smaller. But if the intent is to publish on a regular basis, there should be space for a large light table (page 84) as well as enough elbow room for ten or a dozen people working side by side on production days. Listed below is some of the equipment often found in a small press office.

Sandy Speidel

Light Table

A light table (pages 84-85) is a large illuminated table used for paste-up. It's especially designed with a frosted plate glass top and fitted with fluorescent lights below the glass. On this illuminated surface the flats are placed grid side down. Light passing up through the flats reveals the lines on the backside and allows copy to be centered, justified and evenly pasted down. Probably the cheapest way to acquire a light table is to make it yourself. Construction is simple enough for any Saturday afternoon carpenter. See Worknotes at the end of Chapter VI for details on how to construct one large enough for newspaper work.

IBM Typewriter

The IBM Executive typewriter was introduced back in Chapter VI. Anything larger than an eight-page newspaper is going to call for two of these machines. Renting an Executive during production week or buying one reconditioned is the way to go. Boldface No. 2 is a common and recommended typeface.

The IBM Executive uses a carbon ribbon, much like a strip of carbon paper. It's important that this type of ribbon be used for final copy. A careful look at a page of typed copy from an ordinary machine using a cloth ribbon will reveal a distinct fuzziness resulting from the woven cloth. A fuzzy original can't give a clean, sharp image necessary for good photographic reproduction.

A carbon ribbon, however, passes only once through the machine, doesn't recycle and provides a sharp black image. Other manufacturers make machines with carbon ribbons, but the IBM model is the most common, versatile and reliable. It also offers the widest choice of typefaces. And because it's a popular machine, it's easy to find a shop that will repair, replace, rent or recondition the Executive.

The Executive operates like most typewriters, with key hammers that strike the copy. But as pointed out before, the letters are spaced proportionally, and, when slightly reduced, they approximate a page set in hot type. Otherwise, the machine is little different from an ordinary typewriter.

One thing to watch out for, however, is the Executive's fragile nature.   The keys seem to have a special knack for getting out of alignment.   Misalignment causes the letters to strike too high or low, or appear crooked on the page.   Once in awhile one key will strike harder than the others and perforate the paper.   When renting or buying an Executive, check out the alignment with care before the machine leaves the shop.   If the alignment or anything else, such margin setting, isn't up to snuff, have the machine repaired or find another.   A thing not to do is monkey with the keyboard or try to align the thing yourself.   Unless you have the hands and patience of a little Swiss watchmaker, leave repair work to the experts.

A second typewriter worth considering is the IBM Selectric. The Selectric is not to be confused with the Executive.   This machine has all the type characters on a rotating ball or font.   The beauty of this machine is that typefaces can be changed in a snap, simply by replacing the ball with one of a different type style or size.   The disadvantage of the machine, however, is that the spacing is not proportional. Each letter is allotted the same space as on ordinary typewriters, and the copy off the Selectric definitely lacks the eye appeal of copy produced on an Executive.   But if one of these is available, it's an easy way to add variety to a newspaper or newsletter. Often, an IBM Selectric with an italic ball is used to type letters to the editor, cartoon captions or long quoted paragraphs.

Other Equipment

The light table and IBM typewriters are really the only major expenses involved in setting up a press office. The rest of the equipment and supplies are more or less inexpensive and easy to purchase from office supply stores or from an art supply dealer.

Transfer Lettering, Flexline and Borders

Scout out your local graphic design dealer and get hold of some
of the free catalogs of rub-off lettering supplied by the designer.
Besides transfer headlines, these catalogs show samples of about
twelve zillion different border styles and line options. When using
small hairline or one- and two-point lines (page 101), purchase the kind
that comes on a cellophane backing. Black border tape alone, especially when it approaches hairline, is virtually impossible to lay
down in a straight line. And once it is down, it comes off all too
easily. Flexline printed on cellophane avoids these problems and
is a definite improvement, adhering better than border tape and being
much easier to work with.

When purchasing transfer lettering, stick to one or two type styles
that work well together. Then buy sheets of 18-, 24-, 36-, 42-, and
60-point type. The 24- and 36-point headlines will go the fastest, so
perhaps it's wise to double up on these. Steer away from buying sheets
of oddball styles for only one or two applications. Have patience.
With a little skill and practice transfer headlines can be made fast
and accurately.

T Square

A T square is a very useful device for lining up columns of copy.
Try to find a good metal one 30 inches long. Adjustable wood and
plastic ones can be had, but metal is the most durable and useful.

Rulers and Straight Edges

A printer's ruler, calibrated in picas and inches, is a good investment. Printer's rulers are tough as nails and aren't likely to be
borrowed by amateur carpenters or high school geometry whizzes.
Good too are aluminum and steel rulers with cork backing.

Triangles

A 12-inch, 90-degree plastic triangle is useful for cutting corners.

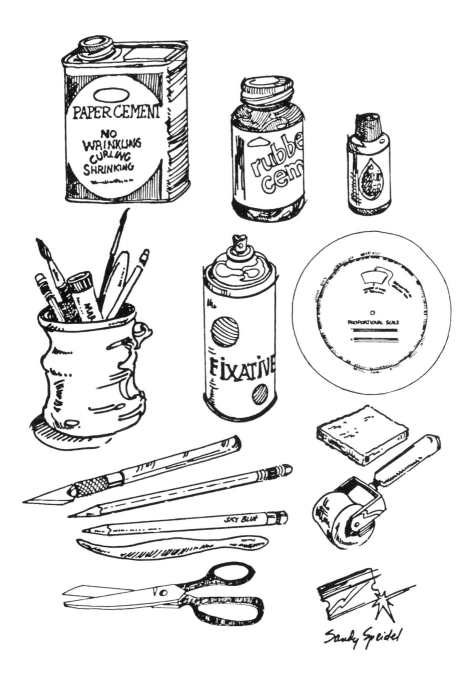

Sandy Speidel

X-acto Knives, Razor Blades

X-acto knives are much easier to work with than razor blades.
They are much safer too. Purchase a half dozen knives and a good
supply of blades. But be forewarned: the blades are expensive and
the knives have a bad habit of disappearing. Keep some industrial
razor blades around, though, but only the kind with one cutting edge.

Scissors

Get some decent ones long enough to be useful. Also get a
cutting board with a large fixed blade.

Rubber Cement

If you're going to use it, buy in quantity -- a quart or more. Get
a supply of thinner also. Be sure to use one-coat cement.

Rubber Cement Pick-Up

A little square of gum rubber that is useful for removing stray
bits of rubber cement, a rubber cement pick-up is sometimes
recommended for removing bits of botched-up transfer lettering.
Don't be without one.

Rubber Cement Pots

Another must, these pots have adjustable brushes that can be
moved up and down with the level of the cement in the pot. The trick
is to put the glue only on the tip of the brush, not on the shaft. These
pots are most helpful in the constant battle to keep rubber cement
from inundating the world.

Tape Dispensers

Transparent tape and masking tape are the two tapes used most
often in preparing layouts. Try to find dispensers which will handle
rolls of either, then buy four or five of them.

Proportional Scale

This scale is a set of two round discs with calibrations on the outer edges. Often called a reduction wheel, this device allows for the calculation of reduction and enlargement percentages for graphics and photos in a flash. For example, if a five-inch cartoon needs to be reduced to three inches to fit a column space, the wheel will tell the size of the reduction. Simply by lining up the original measurement of five inches on one disc and the desired size of three inches on the other, the percentage, in this case 60 percent, is read off a third scale.

Typewriter Correction Fluid

Try Liquid Paper. But get a bottle of thinner and keep the stuff well thinned. Some recommend opaque white ink, others white correction papers. But don't expect any easy or really satisfactory solutions to typewriter corrections.

Blue Pencils

Try them all out and make a choice of brands. An improvement on the blue pencil is the non-photo blue felt tip pen. This is a must when using professional reproduction paper, as the stuff is so hard and slick that it can't be written on with a soft blue pencil.

Paper Cutter

As mentioned above, this is a slicing blade mounted on a board, often used in high school art classes. It's very useful for cutting long, straight edges. See if one can be borrowed or had secondhand before you invest in a new one.

Paper

Shop around for good 8 1/2" x 14" paper, otherwise known as legal size. One thing to look for is smooth surface texture. Lint or excessive texture will cause the copy to appear fuzzy. Duplicator paper will work in a pinch. Reylon or professional reproducing paper is kindest to the camera.

Rollers

Easiest to obtain are hard rubber ink rollers found in art supply stores.   There are special rollers for graphic work.   Wooden and much narrower than ink rollers, these allow you to really elbow down on the copy.

Spray Fixative

A must if you're using professional reproducing paper. It keeps the copy from smearing.

Spray Adhesive

Stick-on stuff in a spray can, spray adhesive is touted as the space age answer to the old rubber cement dilemma.   You can give it a try.

Tracing Paper

Tracing paper is useful in making dummies and also good as a go-between when rolling copy down.

Multi Burnisher

This little plastic device has both a point and a small roller for dealing with transfer lettering.

Small Blackboard

The editorial crew will find this handy for listing copy, determining page allocations and so forth.

Other Useful Items

Other handy tools include bulletin boards; boxes for holding copy; and coffee cans for pencils, rulers and other small items.

The Production Process

Above are some of the tools
and processes described in this
chapter. From upper left and
rotating clockwise, they are:
A light table; composing headlines with rub-off lettering; the
strip printer, also used to make
headlines; and the famous IBM
Executive typewriter. At the
bottom right is a waxing machine
used to fix copy to flats.

The IBM Composer

If you're considering
publishing a newspaper or
a large newsletter on a
regular basis, an improvement on the IBM Executive
typewriter is the IBM
Composer. This beast,
which looks like a space-
age typewriter, combines
the interchangeable print
ball of the familiar IBM
Selectric typewriter with
the proportional spacing
of the Executive. The type ball or font gives you a variety of typefaces
(130) with sizes ranging from 6 to 12 points. Surprisingly, it's almost
as easy to operate as the Executive. The Composer can be used to
justify columns, giving an even right margin, but you have to retype
each line twice to do it. The ball option means you can change from
roman to italic or universal typefaces all on the same machine.

(courtesy IBM)

Although other manufacturers offer similar machines, the IBM
Composer is backed up by a service department that is beyond compare. Naturally, the Composer costs considerably more to rent
or purchase than an Executive. It's a little less than $5,000 new or
around $175 a month to rent. A good used Executive goes for about
$500 these days or about $35 a month to rent. If you do buy a Composer, be sure to get a service contract from IBM because it's a finicky
animal that has to be tweaked often.

Of course, if money is no object since your Aunt Bedilia passed
away and left her prize collection of Titians to be auctioned off, then
you might consider a phototypesetter like a Compugraphic. This
monster comes in various models, ranging in price from about $5,000
to $40,000, and sets clear, sharp, justified copy on a strip of film.
Get in touch with a Compugraphic dealer for more details.

IX
Typography

Headlines should be approached with a wary eye and a focused understanding, for you will soon discover that they are an art form unto themselves. Attractive headlines and typefaces are important because they are most often the chief visual hook into a story. For the reader, casually browsing through your paper or newsletter, they are a peep preview of what's inside.

The discussion of headlines begins with typography or the use of type. Since the mid 1800s American printers have used what's known as a point system to standardize spacing and type sizes. The American point measures .01384 inches or about 1/72 of an inch. Twelve points make up what's called a pica. The pica is the standard unit for horizontal measurement among printers. Thus the pica equals about 1/6 of an inch.

Headline height, and all type for that matter, is measured in point size. Therefore, a 72-point headline is about an inch high, a 36-point headline is about 1/2 inch high, a 12-point headline is three times smaller and so on. But as the illustration on the following page shows, all of this can be very misleading.

Point size is the measurement from the top of the upper-most ascender (the top of a lower case l, b, d, f, or k, for example) on a given type style to the lower-most descender (the bottom edge of the lower case y, j, p, q, or g). Care has to be taken, though. The functional or "true" size of a letter is known as the x-height. The x-height is the height of the primary letters -- the lower case a, o, m or x, for example. The thing to remember is that point size is only an approximation. To the eye, very fat letters appear much larger than those of the same point size which are just styled thinner.

The Point System

The point system is the printer's unit system of measurement. Twelve points make one pica.

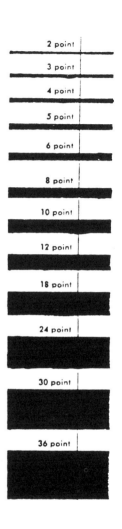

The Deceptive Nature of Point Size

The deceptive nature of point size is illustrated by the two typefaces "xyl," which are the same point size. Even so, the last three letters appear to be much smaller than the first three. This is because point size measures the distance from the top of the l's to the bottom of the y's. Here the true measure of the letter size is the x-height. Here the x-height of the second set of characters is only about 3/4 of the first.

The real key to vertical spacing of headlines is the baseline or bottom of the primary letters. If the front page calls for 48-point type in upper-lower headlines as in the Tan Apartment example on page 54, then the baseline is what determines the centering of the head once the type style has been selected. Many times ascenders and descenders will be of different lengths. With abnormally long descenders, for example, the baseline would be higher than if they were the same length.

Type Styles

Since the invention of movable type by Gutenberg in the mid-15th Century, literally thousands of modifications have been made to the letterforms of the Latin alphabet. In order to compose attractive headlines, it's not necessary to become a walking encyclopedia of typography. But it is a wise idea to become familiar with type systems commonly used in offset publications.

There are six major typefaces, all shown on page 104. But only two of them -- Roman and Monotone -- are commonly used for composing headlines. The other four, Text, Square Serif, Written and Ornamental, are seen occasionally in newspapers. When they are used, it's almost always in the banner or advertising copy.

The first and oldest face is the Roman. Roman letters are characterized by serifs, the tiny feet on the ends of the main stroke, and also the elegant swelling and thinning in the curved portions of the letterform. In ancient Rome, these letters were developed by the stonecutter and often decorated the facades of buildings. The stone medium and mason's chisel dictated a lot of the refinements of the lettering. For example, there was great danger of the stone crumbling at the T intersection of the main stroke of the serif. So here the cutter carefully rounded off the corners and bracketed the serif to the main stroke.

Roman letters come in two major subdivisions: Old Style and

TYPE FACES

Roman		
	Old Style	**ABCDEabcdefg**
	Modern	ABCDEFabcde
Monotone		
	Sans Serif	**ABCDabcde**
	Gothic	ABCDEabcdef
Text		𝕬𝕭𝕮𝕯𝕰𝖆𝖇𝖈𝖉𝖊𝖋𝖌𝖍𝖎
Square		
	Egyptian	**ABCDEabcde**
	American	**ABCDEFGHIabcdefghi**
Written		
	Cursive	ABCDEFGHIabcdefghijkl
	Script	𝒜ℬ𝒞𝒟ℰabcdefgh
Ornamental		
	Shaded	ABCDEF
	Shadowed	ABCDEFGHIJL
	Novelty	ABCDEFGH

Modern.   These distinctions get blurry, but Old Style Romans are heftier than their Modern counterparts. Also the thinnest area of the letterform -- in an e or an o for example -- occurs not at the top or bottom but rather slightly before, at 11 and 5 o'clock.   Thus the Old Style Roman letters are on an axis which tips to the left.

Modern Roman, on the other hand, has letterforms which are much thinner than Old Style.   The narrowest areas of the letters occur at 12 and 6 o'clock, thus resulting in a vertical axis.   The classic Modern Roman is Bodoni, which graces the front page headlines of the GRAPEVINE.   There are all sorts of variations, but Modern Roman is recognized easily by its vertical axis, thin fine strokes and tiny serifs.

Italic is a variation of Roman which leans to the right. Italics were first developed about 1500 in an effort to approximate written script.   They come in both Roman Modern and Old Style.

The second important face is the Monotone.   Like the Roman, Monotone comes in two basic divisions: Gothic and Sans Serif. But these guys are even more difficult for non-experts to tell apart than their Roman cousins. In fact, printers often add to confusion themselves by lumping them all together.   The distinctions are blurred indeed, but the face itself is easy to spot.   This is because all Monotones come without serifs.

Gothic letters are the same width throughout and do not have any of the elegance associated with Roman letterforms.   The type was named after the barbarian hordes which terrorized Europe, not after the cathedral architecture.   The term translates as "ugly."

The Sans Serifs are very similar but somewhat more rounded than the Gothic. Their letters may be slightly narrowed where curves meet vertical strokes. Check out the d's in the example. The distinctions, admittedly, are slight.

The remaining faces are not so commonly used. They include Text, often mistakenly called Old English.   Text is handy on nameplates or obituaries. Elsewhere, it would seem out of place.

Then there are the Square Serifs and the Egyptian and American squares. The Egyptian has serifs the same size as the body strokes. On its American counterpart, the serifs are even larger than the body strokes. Egyptian type can be useful at times as a letterhead. But one is left to ponder where American Square type might be used, other than decorating circus wagons and bar fronts.

Likewise, written letterforms are seldom of value in small newspapers or newsletters. This face comes in two general subdivisions: Script, in which the letters are joined, and Cursive, in which the letters are not strung together.

The final face we'll talk about is Ornamental. Two subdivisions that can be put to occasional use are the shaded and shadowed letterforms. Shaded lettering is used on the <u>GRAPEVINE</u> nameplate. Shadowed lettering is also often used the same way. Novelty type makes up the last subdivision. These faces can be useful in advertising.

Typefaces are forever being modified in weight, height and angle. But even so, the basic style of the face remains the same. Weight has to do with the thickness of the strokes used to make a letter. Thus a skinny letter is referred to as light and its heavier counterpart of the same family is termed heavy, black, bold or even ultrabold. Another twist is to squeeze the letters together: Then they are said to be condensed. Likewise, stretching a letter out horizontally results in an extended face. There are even such things as backslant faces which tilt to the left.

Headline Composition

Writing a good headline is easier to talk about than to actually do. As anyone who has spent a couple of long nights suffering the tedium of a composing room will tell you, headlines are a special pain in the neck that demand a special talent. Their composition usually takes time. Following are a number of guidelines that should prove useful when composing headlines.

1)   Headlines should be vital and in the present tense. This means
use an active verb whenever possible. For example:

CITY POLICE JAIL STREET ARTISTS

or simply:

STREET ARTISTS JAILED

Both are good examples of simple, active, informative, action-
potential headlines that could be used in a banner fashion or
over a single column.

2)   Heads should be idiomatic, that is, closer to spoken language,
and have an unstilted, natural quality.   Reading a headline out
loud is a good test. If the head sounds good, it's probably okay.
Here's an example of a headline which may at first look acceptable, but flunks the out loud test.

LOCAL AUTHORITIES CITE STREET VENDORS
AT UNIVERSITY AVENUE CONFRONTATION

Even with enough space on the layout, this doesn't make it. It's
too long, it's stilted and unnatural and it doesn't pack the wallop
of the original. Imagine someone running up to you on the street
mouthing this monster. Sure, you might see the likes of it in the
Wall Street Journal, but it would be poor use in a community paper.
This is because the immediacy of the conflict -- the life and the
breathing essence of the story -- has been extracted in our long-
winded example. It's this very vitality and immediacy that is the
secret of a successful independent newspaper.

3) Keep headlines simple. Again the direct approach is usually the
    best. Heads should be uncluttered with neither too much punctua-
    tion nor too many words. The confusion rendered in the following
    abomination should demonstrate why.

    SIDEWALK ' UNSUITABLE, ' SAYS P.A. COUNCIL
    VENDORS TOLD: 'MOVE ... OR FACE ARREST'

    Why not be more straightforward and write the headline like this:

    COUNCIL TELLS STREET ARTISTS TO MOVE ALONG

    And if quotes must be used, try a single quote mark.

4) Straplines or "kickers" are sometimes useful to help explain a
    headline as shown below.

    On University Avenue
    STREET ARTISTS FACE ARREST

5) With two- or three-line heads, construction proceeds phrase by
    phrase, especially if the heads exceed more than one column.

    ALBATROSS PRESS IS
    A GOOD LOCAL PAPER

    THE ALBATROSS PRESS
    IS A GOOD LOCAL PAPER

    Avoid ending lines with words like "THE," "A," "THAT."
    Remember, too, that the whole sense of a headline can be altered
    by faulty phrasing or omission of punctuation as is amply demon-
    strated in the following examples:

DISABLED FLY
TO SEE PRESIDENT

GENERALS FLY
BACK TO FRONT

Consider yourself warned.

6)   Misuse of the word said and of modifiers are two of the most
common faults in large American newspapers.   Shun the
following type of headline phrasing:

LOCAL CLINIC SAID BROKE

COUNCILMAN BLAKE SAID CORRUPT

30 MILLION CIGARS SMOKED

A simple solution is to fill in the missing who.   For example:

Review Board Reports
LOCAL CLINIC GOING BROKE

   CITY ATTORNEY CHARGES
COUNCILMAN BLAKE CORRUPT

AMERICANS YEARLY SMOKE
   30 MILLION CIGARS

7)   Note the different structure in the last three examples.   The two
decks of the first example are left justified at the column edge.
This is a simple, time-tested approach to laying down headlines.

It may also be one of the easiest methods for a burgeoning independent newspaper to duplicate with the least amount of hassle.
But be forewarned, if used to excess it tends to give the paper
a blocky appearance and is best used in conjunction with other
headline formats.

The second example, though infrequently used, is acceptable.
In this case the accusation that councilman Blake is corrupt is
certainly the essence of the headline, but to be complete, it must
also contain reference to the city attorney. With the given word
choice there is no other way to easily chop this example in two
decks. Our Councilman Corrupt headline can be arranged like
the Local Clinic example, but it can't be pasted down like the 30
Million Cigars headline.

The last headline is a simple inverted pyramid format. It's
a good construction for independent newspapers and will mix well
with the first example's left-justified format. Its advantages
include its symmetry, its tendency to pull the eye downward, and
the pleasing white space left by the second or subsequent decks.
The only disadvantage is it may not be possible to compose one
of these every time you'd like to.

For examples of this type of inverted head in the extreme, see
copies of the New York Times circa 1948. Though elegant, these
leave the curious to ponder: did anyone ever really appreciate
such elaborate headlines?

Keep in mind that there is such a thing as a too perfectly laid
out page. Variety is essential in every aspect of a newspaper,
headlines included. Two or three standard and well-chosen typefaces and a variation of headline formats will interest readers,
pull them into the copy and go a long way in relieving the tedium
of too much print.

8) Don't use words like "he" or "they" in headlines. Tell the reader exactly who or what the story is about. If Father Juniper was locked out of his church after his indiscretions with the organist were discovered by the Vicar, the headline should say as much.

9) In general don't use exclamation   marks anywhere. They don't add anything to a headline and are seldom useful in the text.

10) The overall shape of a headline is important. A headline can be a turnoff simply because it looks bad. The usual arrangement for centered headlines is long-short-long-short, tapering at the end to the shortest line. But if the headlines are justified on the left, short-long-short-long becomes the rule.

11) On feature pages or in articles with lots of pictures or graphics, the visuals determine the makeup and the layout proceeds around them. In these cases, many of the normal rules for headlines can be ignored as the pictures become the visual hook. Again, being straightforward is a good rule of thumb. Don't clutter up a good photo feature with irrelevant headlines.

12) Beware of headlinese. Words like "ban," "bid," "probe," "hits," "Red," "kill" put millions to sleep everyday in the established daily press. You're supposed to be an independent alternative, remember?

13) Try to spark the reader's imagination with anything that will lure the mind to that forbidding lump of print. But while doing so, be sure to be accurate. Don't overstate the case or focus on an issue of the story which is not the main news point.

14) Make headlines as complete as possible in the allotted space. Be specific, eye-catching, to the point. Avoid the vague and general.

Centering Headlines

Taking the mystery out of centering headlines is accomplished by
a process known as "counting in," that is, taking a character count of
a prospective headline. By counting in before composing a head, you
can be sure that it will fit.

Mechanically, counting in involves taking a unit total of all the characters and spaces between words in a proposed headline. Then, the
units are added up to assure that the headline will be the right size
for the allotted dimensions on the copy page. Regardless of whether
heads are set in hot type, photographically by strip printer or Veri-
type or with transfer lettering, the count-in method can be used. The
system is not foolproof and varies with different styles of typefaces,
but it usually works in the following manner:

A character count is achieved by simply assigning one unit of
space to every lowercase letter, except l, i, f, t, and j. These are
thin letters and are assigned half a unit because they're skinny. The
letters w and m get one and one half units because they are fat. Capitals
follow the same general rule only each character is half a unit larger
than its lowercase counterpart. Numbers and the space between two
words are one unit and punctuation marks are a half. It sounds more
complicated than it really is. The following example shows how the
formula works in practice.

1 1 1 1 1 1 ½ ½ 1 1½ ½ = 8

on scott st.

POLICE BUST ARTISTS

1½ 1½ 1½ 1 1½ 1½ 1 1 ½ 1 1½ 1½ 1 1½ 1½ 1½ 1 1½ 1½ 1½   = 26 1/2

Keep in mind that all typefaces are not counted the same. Therefore, it's necessary to be quite familiar with the style that your newspaper regularly uses. Corresponding letters in one typeface may be
fat and occupy more space than the same letters in a different style.

From here, all that is necessary to know is the number of units per column width for each size and style of typeface used on your paper.

A good way to familiarize the people doing layout with the various headline styles and options available is to clip and mount the different styles side by side and display them conspicuously by point size in the copy room. At first, it may be necessary to consult the chart often, but soon regulars on the pasteup staff will learn the headline options by heart and the pace of production will pick up accordingly.

Worknotes

Boxed headlines often become a disaster on a small newspaper. The safest way to keep them from turning your paper into a scream sheet is to use thin lines and stay away from solid boxes.

LETTERS

Aren't the last three a lot more attractive? So, as a rule, lay off the heavy lines unless you want your paper to look like the National Enquirer.

LETTERS

STAFF

STAFF

X
Staff Organization

Leaflets and newsletters may be produced by a single individual or a couple of people working together. But to publish an entire newspaper on a regular basis requires a staff. Whether large or small, a staff requires coordination. This means it usually falls to one person to hold all the pieces of an issue together, right down to the moment of printing. Copy has to be gathered, researched and edited. Deadlines must be set and adhered to; bills paid; supplies purchased; photos taken and developed; copy typeset, proofed and pasted up, etc. Who looks after the entire issue before it goes to the printer? Who picks up that ton of newsprint at the press? How does it get distributed to the community?

Traditionally, newspapers are organized with a top-down structure. Under this system, the managing editor seems to wind up with all the say on a day-to-day basis. But for many independent or volunteer papers this isn't a satisfactory blueprint. Many of them desire more flexibility and seek to break out of what they view as a constraining, antiquated system. This effort to redistribute responsibility to a more egalitarian base is more than just a philosophical whim. It can make a lot of sense organizationally. Motivated people sharing responsibility for all phases of newspaper production (including the tedious jobs) can jointly achieve the common goal -- an imaginative, informative publication.

Structured Staff Rotation

Sounds great, but just how is all this accomplished? Well, one answer is structured rotation. That is, positions of responsibility and control, such as membership on the editorial board, are rotated on a regular schedule. On a small paper staff rotation serves a number of purposes.

First, it ensures that no single person or small elite gains too much control over the newspaper. Next, and perhaps more important, it provides an organizational training ground for the larger community. Thus, by using this type of approach, community members who haven't had access to a fancy education are offered a chance to learn not only news reporting and publications skills, but also group organization and bureaucratic methods which they normally have little other way of acquiring. Finally, staff rotation combats the boogeyman of "burnout" which stalks every volunteer group. So we find a rotating structure helps fight burnout, encourages people to take time off and guards against intellectual stagnation and accompanying loss of purpose, imagination and motivation.

Setting Up an Independent Newspaper

Let's assume a small, ambitious group of diverse people scraped together enough money to launch an independent newspaper. For them, the money angle was not so difficult. In a short period of time they hustled up a couple of low-interest loans, got a small grant from a local foundation interested in community groups and shook down a few liberal professors and businesspeople.

The immediate goal was to produce a sample four-page first edition with a few illustrative articles to publicize their existence. They also intended to announce a general staff recruiting meeting open to all members of the community.

The task ahead seemed at first straightforward enough. All they had to do was print and distribute a few thousand sample copies, find themselves a regular meeting place and continue to encourage local partici-

pation. But even as they set out to do this, other questions began to
plague them. Some were obvious: Where were they going to find
a press? How were they going to learn everything they needed to
know about printing and distributing a newspaper? Once they did
master the mechanics of putting a paper together, what bushes would
they have to beat to get all the inside low-down on the community?
In short, how would they, as a relatively inexperienced and loosely
structured organization, come up with well-written and documented in-
vestigative stories that rivaled the best in the larger papers?

There was broad agreement about the paper to be sure. It was
to be a monthly at first, reflecting the group's interests in social change
with their in-depth reporting of local political and cultural issues. There
were plans to cover city hall and the board of supervisors, investigate
conditions in the county jail and so forth. A good deal of copy would
be given to such topics as child care, women's and minority rights,
establishing a community medical clinic, the uphill struggles of independent businesses and craftspeople, democratic participation in community planning and the like.

But while producing the very first issue, a number of unforeseen
problems popped up. For example, no one had really thought out
how, and by whom, copy would be edited. Just what in concrete terms
was the newspaper's political slant, anyway? Was there anything that
they couldn't or wouldn't print? If so, what? Or take the issue of paid
advertising. Was there any kind of advertising which they wouldn't
accept? The staff quickly split on this question. Half of them thought
they should take any kind of advertising, the other half wanted to set
up specific guidelines. Then, if they did decide to run lots of advertising, who was going to keep track of the whole financial angle ?

After a couple of exhausting meetings full of questions and doubts,
our friends began to address some of these problems. With a lot of
head scratching, they set down and painfully worked out a system

to meet their needs. To begin with, they examined the makeup of
the staff.

Most of the staff on the paper, they realize, would not be paid.
Hopefully, a handful in the future might draw token salaries, but in
order for the paper to fly, the bulk of the work would be done with
volunteers. Thus the backbone of the paper would be a diverse group
of hardworking people ranging in age from their early twenties to
their late fifties. Many were working folks. Others were young semi-
professionals or professionals not entirely satisfied with their lives.
A few once attended a large local university. One or two had a long
history of community involvement or anti-war activity from the Vietnam
era. Yet no single group, individual or point of view dominated the staff.

For these and other reasons the paper decided to project a deliberately liberal image. Most on the staff who thought of themselves
as progressives agreed that the paper should be designed for those
people they were trying to reach, in this case the liberal, reformist
and progressive sections of the community.

In the past, two staff members had been involved in publishing a
militant community paper structured along doctrinaire lines. They
soon discovered that few people in the community could relate to it.
As a consequence, it was not read or taken seriously. People com-
plained, among other things, that they didn't see how such broad, sweep-
ing analysis related to their daily lives. Thus there was real experience
to learn from and our group resolved to design the paper around the
real needs of the community, not what they personally thought the needs
ought to be.

Those on the staff with a progressive outlook understood from experience that it would be necessary to get many diverse people involved
in this as well as other community projects before any substantial or
meaningful change would be brought about. They knew investigating,
muckraking, and encouraging grassroots groups to take action were all

worthwhile efforts.   Pushing for social change involved more than talking among themselves, they concluded. If the paper was going to
effectively do what they wanted it to, it had to reflect a varied con-
stituency and relate to people in terms that they understood.

Besides this core of progressive and committed people, there
were twice as many members who functioned on
the paper on a less regular basis.   Some were
occasionally staff writers, others showed up now
and then to edit , help out with the pasteup and
socialize.   Others came only to type copy and
lay out advertising. Yet after a while, on any
single given issue, the staff box of the new paper would contain anywhere from 35 to 50 contributors.

Team Structure

At first, "do your own thing" and collective
anarchy seemed to be the new paper's policy.
A crazy quilt of inconsistencies, spotty news
coverage and shoddy layout was the published
result. One month a nihilist debate and dynamite society bulldozed an article through the
unstructured staff which concluded that the only
sure way to change anything was to murder the
rich in their beds. The next month a five thousand word plea by the World Peace and Love
Brotherhood urged readers to besiege Western
Union and wire flowers to Russia protesting
the exile of an 88-year-old Estonian poet
to the Siberian steppe.

For a while, it seemed that the

new paper filled its sails with just about any wind which blew hard enough. Not surprisingly, the general appearance of the paper vacillated like a storm-tossed weathervane. Some issues looked great. Others might have been put to better use as fish wrappers. After a short while, it became painfully obvious that the paper would have to chart a consistent course if for no other reason than to be taken seriously. To this end, the whole staff concluded that a more structured approach was necessary. It opted to delegate overall authority to an editorial board to ensure consistency. But at the same time it feared the constraints of a top-down bureaucracy. So to solve this problem, the staff decided to rotate editorial positions on a regular basis. A functioning team system was what evolved.

The team system didn't drop from the sky. It came from experience and was a painfully debated and well-reasoned solution to real problems which plagued the paper after a haphazard beginning. Thus, the big dilemma that was tackled and eventually resolved was how to remedy the lack of coherence in content and at the same time make the visuals, such as photos and line drawings, consistent. The new system was tried out for two issues. Everyone concluded that the novel team approach, which interlocked with a rotating editorial board, well suited the paper's needs. The system worked this way:

Each team would select a team leader to coordinate its affairs. The leader would serve on that issue's editorial board. In turn, the board was orchestrated by a person given the title of coordinator for the issue. The editorial board had final say over what went into each issue. Yet the ultimate authority resided in the collective decisions of the teams. They researched, wrote and edited the copy and chose the team member who would represent them on the editorial board.

At both the team and editorial levels, formal votes were rarely taken. Most problems were resolved by consensus. Those that couldn't be resolved to everyone's satisfaction were taken up at the monthly general meeting when the new overall coordinator was chosen.

A Brief Run Through The System

Let's take a look at the evolution of a story from scratch, tracing it through the mini-bureaucracy of our independent newspaper.

Mary Beth, an elementary school teacher who spends her spare hours painting water colors, came home one day to discover that she and her housemates were to be evicted from their funky old Victorian home on High Street. It seemed that the property was being sold and rezoned for high-density clapboard apartments. It was also suspected that at least two members of the city council, who were real estate brokers, stood to clean up financially if the deal went through. So Mary Beth telephoned our independent community newspaper, hoping it might be interested in the three-page story she had drafted.

She was in luck. The voice on the other end of the line told her to contact Emmylou, who was team leader for local news. Emmylou suggested that Mary Beth come to the next team meeting Thursday night, but in the meantime to call Bill who had covered the city council beat in the past. Bill turned out to be a real help. He not only promised to look over Mary Beth's copy but also gave her leads on how to research public records and documents pertinent to her story. That Thursday, at the team meeting, Bill introduced Mary Beth to the rest of the team and explained briefly how he believed certain council members stood to make thousands off the High Street evictions and rezoning. It seemed that the first council member's real estate firm stood to make a killing on the construction agreement, and the second council member's brother-in-law was bidding to purchase the condemned property.

At the meeting, the team reviewed Mary Beth's copy. They scribbled comments in the margins and made suggestions on the back. The team liked the story but suggested some minor changes and deletions. Meanwhile, Fred, who had experience with cameras, offered to photograph the houses marked for demolition.

A few days later, the reworked story and the photographs went once

more to Emmylou. She took this final version, along with the rest
of the team's stories, to the editorial board meeting. The editorial
board looked over the copy briefly, debated its merits and priority,
and assigned space on the second page of the upcoming issue to accommodate the article and photograph.

Later that week, Emmylou called Mary Beth back to tell her the
good news. She invited her to come and help type and paste up the
final version of the story. Mary Beth showed up Saturday afternoon
and, along with the other members of the team, took part in the layout of her own story.

By the middle of the following week, Mary Beth's article was on the
streets. She even distributed a few dozen copies herself. Before
Friday, the city council members were issuing heated denials and the
larger papers had picked up on the story. On Saturday, a local ac-
tivist lawyer called up Mary Beth and offered to fight the evictions.

Looking at Traditional Newspaper Structures

Newspapers are historically mechanisms of political power. The
traditional structure of a newspaper staff over the years is to have a
chief executive, called an editor or editor-in-chief, at the top. One
of the many tasks of the editor is to ride herd over a staff of editorial
writers and determine the posture of the newspaper towards political
and economic issues. As representative of the stockholders and owners, the editor functions to set the boundaries of political discussion
and debate. In short, an editor is the person through whom control of
the paper is maintained by the owners and publishers.

Think of the editor as a sort of political gatekeeper or policy honcho
who keeps house for the owners and determines the "slant" of the paper.
Once understood, this goes a long way towards explaining the structure
of traditional newspapers. It's the editor who decides who to endorse
in the elections, which side to take in labor disputes and whether or not

the paper will side with the current Washington fad in foreign policy. Seldom active in the day-to-day operation of the newsroom, the editor-in-chief occupies a position deliberately removed and detached from the everyday running of the newspaper.

The Managing Editor

Looking deeper, one discovers the real kingpin who coordinates the daily workings of a newspaper, the managing editor. This person is in charge of the entire news field from feature reporting to photography. A managing editor judges the importance of a story, where it's placed and the headline makeup. This editor's responsibilities extend to the overall coordination of the various departments and the administration of tasks which ensure the smooth operation of a daily newspaper. Assembled under the managing editor are numerous other editors, the most important of these being the city editor and the news editor.

The city editor is in charge of all the city and local news. Working out of the city desk are usually several assistants and reporters. Key among these assistants is the assignment person, who spends most of the day trailing reporters around on the phone, directing them and instructing the work in the field. Other assistants edit and compile the local news and rework the reporters' stories for publication.

Then there is the news editor. All regular news copy passes over this person's desk. The editor determines the headline size and the composition and placement of each news story and also compiles a list of news items for each issue. Rough dummies for the copy team are also prepared at this stage. After approval by various editors, department heads and directors, the copy goes to a copydesk. There it's given a final reading and copy editing. The copyreader, in addition to proofing copy, works out headlines and subheads as ordered by the news editor. Finally, the copy is whisked off to the composing room and typeset.

In the composing room, the layout editor prepares to paste up the copy, working from the news editor's dummies. It's the layout editor's job to physically fix the news copy, features, photographs and graphics in the paper in an attractive, consistent and well-balanced arrangement. The decisions of both the news editors and layout editor are subject to the approval of the managing editor.

Looking at a large newspaper setup still closer, one discovers wire editors, sports editors, fashion editors, financial editors, women's page editors, art editors, Sunday editors, etc. Each of these bailiwicks has a group of reporters, special writers and copyreaders under them. The larger papers have staffs of specialized writers who work only on Sunday features, society news, theaters, movies, books or television.

In addition, this machine may include various executives and assistants, critics, columnists, staff correspondents, foreign liaisons, an exchange editor and a morgue librarian. A single person is often in charge of the wire services, and there can be a brigade of comic and sketch artists, photographers, copy runners, etc.

With all this, there still remains one other domain requiring special mention. Many times the business department is organized apart from the rest of the paper, the commercial management being entirely divorced from the news end. Advertising may also have its own staff and management to handle display, classified and want ads. Sometimes the business end will also include a circulation manager, someone who is given the job of overseeing distribution of the paper to dealers and subscribers. There can even be a promotion department devoted solely to promoting the paper's interests and increasing its readership.

Obviously, this level of complexity is not required on a small paper, and many of the tasks described above can be combined into the duties of a single person. Yet to effectively produce a newspaper, it's wise to follow a similar structure and production routine. This is because newspaper production has developed into an exact science over decades of practice. Happily, the right way is most often the quickest and easiest way in almost every case. This isn't to say that innovation should be discouraged. Initiative and originality are always in demand. But what it does mean is that a framework has to be constructed for burgeoning literary genius to plug into. In brief, somebody has to be put in charge.

So it was to this end that our small independent paper devised its rotating team and editorial structure. We opted to make a coordinator responsible for getting the issue of the paper out on time each month. This person also supervised each step of the paper's production from gathering the news and editing it to reading the final copy. And all the work did not fall to the coordinator; instead, the coordinator concentrated on spreading out the work and making sure that everything was done properly. When hard decisions had to be made, it was the coordinator's job to consult all the members of the editorial board and make sure that the puzzle pieces of the issue all fit together in the end.

Generally, the coordinator was someone who was well-liked and diplomatic but also decisive when need be. The job required writing ability and a capacity for work -- often more than a fair share. Moreover, the coordinator had to be able to delegate authority and work in an effective manner so as to not get snared into tackling everything single-handedly. If the issue required an editorial, more times than not the coordinator was the person who wrote it. In addition, the coordinator had to have an eye for a well-written news story and enough artistic savvy to be able to distinguish a balanced page from an unbalanced one. Then there was one last very important item. The coordinator had to have lots of enthusiasm.

Working together with the coordinator were the team leaders. They also had writing and editing skills. They gathered the news from the team members, saw to it that the copy was properly edited, made up headlines, read the proofs and supervised the team layout and pasteup.

So our small independent newspaper was able to work out its organizational problems with a system tailored to meet its particular needs. The rotating editorial board and team structure gave us a centralized system which was deliberately designed loosely enough to encourage participation by anyone with the energy to tackle team problems.

As a result, overtime, copy content and news coverage became more consistent. The paper's readership picked up. New, eager and enthusiastic faces appeared at the monthly meetings. And most important, there was a place for new people and a structure they could plug into.

Worknotes

Organization: Staff organization is the most difficult part of putting out a community newspaper. Try to develop a bootstrap mentality and always consider the long haul. Start thinking in terms of years rather than next Tuesday's deadline.

Overambition: Beware of overambition. Have a clear idea of what you can or cannot produce. Unrealistic goals can place an unfair burden on the group. Hard workers deserve a break,too, or they will burn out. Fight this problem by enforced rotation of those who do more than their fair share.

Training: Make training and teaching a top priority. This takes more time in the beginning, but pays off in the end. Rotating positions of responsibility allows people to acquire skills in group coordination that they may have no other way of obtaining. With little money and a heavy reliance on volunteers, producing experienced community activists can be as vital as the contents of the paper itself.

Leaders: Leadership should be geared to training others in community newswork so that they can gradually take over more responsibility. In every group there are one or two people who have a clear idea of what they want and how to get it. Often these people have more skill, time and energy than others. Such people can be a tremendous advantage to a group, or they can dominate and stifle it, eventually leading to disaster.

Leaders tend to fall into two general categories: organizers and managers. Organizers are concerned with increasing community participation and spreading out the work, while managers are task-oriented problem solvers who usually do the work themselves. Beware. The two personalities often don't mix. The reason for this is that the organizer is forever experimenting, innovating and attempting to spread out the work in what very often ends up a chaotic and unwieldy arrangement. Organizers see their job as putting a fire under people, sparking their imagination, enthusiasm and participation. A good manager, on the other hand, often goes around snuffing out such sparks of inspiration because of the need to control, channel, pigeon-hole and bureaucratize.

It's best for everyone that a clear strategy and purpose be mapped out. The goals of the newspaper should be clearly agreed upon and a satisfactory organizational structure set up before publication begins. The structure should be loose enough for others to join and modify if necessary. Good leaders work to replace and duplicate themselves. So put them to work training others in writing, editing and layout.

Decision Making: Voting is the menu, not the meal, as the old saying goes. Most people are not accustomed to exercising direct control over their institutions. This lack of control heavily influences how they view decision making. Occasionally we vote for elected representatives and defer to them the power to make decisions that affect our lives. But when that meal we voted on arrives and it's not to our taste, about all we retain is the right to grumble about our own lousy judgment.

General meetings can work as decision-making bodies only if they are not too large. The larger the meeting becomes, the more likely it is to be a ratifying body which vetoes or approves decisions made by an editorial board or informal caucus.

Informal decision making is often more important than a formal vote. In most groups the most active people often informally discuss problems among themselves, reaching tentative solutions and then placing the item on the agenda for the general meeting.   There is nothing inherently wrong with informal decision making as long as the process is open to all and minority opinions are respected.   Perhaps the biggest pitfall is that the process will become monopolized by a closed inner clique or elite.   But if this is guarded against and the process is open to all, influence tends to be proportional to a person's active participation in a group.

XI
Circulation, Advertising
and Money Matters

So you've decided to publish a small community newspaper or news-letter. But unless the paper is subsidized by a school or philanthropic organization, it's probably going to be a squeeze each month to pay the printer. Right from the start there are a number of items which need to be resolved. These include:

-- How often will the paper be published? Once a month? Every week? Biweekly? When this is established, then on what day of the week or days of the month will it be circulated?

-- Will the paper be free to readers or will you charge for it? If you charge for it what will be the newsstand price? What will be the subscription rate?

-- Will it be distributed via newsstands, through street vendors, in shops and businesses or by direct home delivery? If you decide to mail it directly to homes, will it be with a second-class permit, at the third-class bulk rate or with a paid-circulation rate?

When to Publish

For a weekly, Thursday is the most common day to come out. Some papers choose Wednesdays, others Friday. This is primarily to bene-fit the advertisers because they want to take advantage of heavy shopping on weekends. For a monthly, the first weekday of the month is an ob-

vious candidate. Likewise, a biweekly usually comes out around the
first and the fifteenth.

One fly in the ointment may well be your printer's schedule. You
are certain not to be the printer's biggest or most important account
so don't be surprised if you're not able to go to press on the exact
day you'd like to. Regardless, it's important to establish a consistent schedule and stick to it. So try to work out a regular day of the
week or days of the month for going to press.

To Charge or Not to Charge

Will the paper be free to readers or will you charge for it? This
is something to consider carefully. A free newspaper has lots of advantages. For one, it relieves you of the time-consuming burden of
waiting at locked newsstands and collecting small sums of cash from
smokeshops and grocery store consignments. It also frees you of the
headache of bookkeeping for what at best will be only about a quarter
of your revenue. Even on the best paid-circulation papers, the take from
subscriptions and newsstand sales is dwarfed by that of advertising, which
can be expected to bring in about three quarters of the overall income. An
additional advantage of a free paper is the high circulation figure. For
better or worse you will soon discover that merchants and business
people are most often impressed by a large circulation figure. It's
not unreasonable to assume that the loss in revenue suffered by not
charging for the paper can be easily made up with the increased advertising attracted by a large circulation.

On the other hand, there are very good arguments to be made for
charging for the paper. The first of these is the avoidance of the stigma
of junk mail and the advertising throwaway. Many people tend to feel
unless something is paid for, it's not worth reading. For this reason
alone a paper may suffer in esteem, making paid circulation something
to carefully consider. But probably the biggest argument in favor of
paid circulation has to do with the fact that only paid papers qualify for
second-class mailing rates and legal advertising.

Of course, if you do decide to charge for the paper, you will have

to decide how much will be its newsstand price.   This will depend to
some extent on the relative affluence of your reading public as well
as what the competition charges.   Most small papers charge $5 to $10
for a year's subscription and 25 or 35 cents a copy on the newsstand.
The subscription rate, of course, should give a substantial discount over
the newsstand price.

Distribution and Circulation

As mentioned above, mailing the paper is one viable means of distribution.   This is especially true if it qualifies for a second-class
permit.   Free papers are not eligible for the low second-class permit
rate, but a paid circulation paper can expect to pay from 1.5 cents
to 5 cents per piece depending on weight and destination.   A free paper most likely will have to go third class.   This costs about 8.5 cents
for the first ounce after you have paid a $60 annual fee.   Alternatively,
up to two ounces can be mailed third class for 20 cents per piece without the fee.   If the primary means of distribution is going to be mailing, then it will serve you well to look into the postal regulations dealing
with second-class privileges.   Keep in mind that only legitimate paid-
circulation papers qualify and you may well be requested to produce
your subscription records.   Next, the second-class permit has to be
approved in Washington, D. C.   Finally, there is an annual fee of $30
to $120, based on the circulation numbers.   Along the way, also be
ready to produce sample issues, as the postal authorities will want
to see them.

In addition to second- and third-class rates, there is something called
controlled circulation rates which are higher than second-class but
lower than third-class rates.   To qualify for these your paper must
have at least 24 pages, but need not have a paid circulation.   Again
check with your postmaster for details.

Besides direct mailing, there are other, more traditional methods
of circulating a newspaper.   These include use of newsstands, distribution through shops and businesses on consignment, use of street
vendors and direct home delivery.   If your community is compact and

homogeneous,   then all the above methods can be used effectively.

Newsstands can be purchased outright or leased, or you can make
them yourself. When using newsstands, remember that placement
is important and that they should be put in locations where large numbers
of people are accustomed to congregating or areas where other newsstands are located. There are probably not a lot of such locations,
so most likely it will be easy to stock and deliver to the newsstands
yourself.

Convincing local merchants to distribute your paper in their shops
is usually pretty easy if the paper is free. If you charge for it, distribution will have to be on a consignment basis, with the distributor re-
ceiving between 30 and 40 percent of the cover price for copies sold.
When using this method of distribution, try to have the paper displayed
prominently near the front door or even on a corner of the checkout
counter if at all possible.

For paid-circulation papers, use of street vendors is yet another
way of distributing the paper. Here the vendor acts as a free agent,
buying the paper at a discounted rate and pocketing the printed price
when sold on the street corners. Unsold copies are returned and the
vendor is credited with that number of copies towards the next issue.

Direct home delivery is another popular way of distributing in a
compact community. This is especially effective if the paper is one
for which there is no charge, making it subject to high third-class
mailing rates. Here delivery people are hired to go from door to
door, leaving a copy of the paper at each house. An important thing
to note when opting for this method of circulation is that it is illegal
to place the paper directly inside mailboxes.

Advertising

Selling display advertising is never easy. It takes infinite patience
and persistence. Even if the community is blessed with a large and
thriving business section, it's invariably an uphill battle to get them to
advertise. Although the pleasant folks running the funky health food

restaurant or handcrafted leather and pottery shop may dig your paper, it still can be frustratingly hard work to convince them to take out an ad.

One reason for this is the common notion that advertising's more or less a waste, or at best a necessary expense like the gas bill. Another is that facing the competitive hype of the business world each day causes merchants to be suspicious of being high-pressured into buying advertising that they do not want or need. Given all this, selling advertising can be a challenging affair indeed.

GRAPEVINE

P. O. Box 11572, Palo Alto, California 94306

We would like to acquaint you with The Grapevine, the Midpeninsula's only community-access newspaper. The Grapevine is published monthly by people from the community to express the opinions and interests of ordinary folks as we cope with these unusual times.

We are in our fourth year of publication, with a circulation of 12,000 and growing, in an area from Redwood City to Mountain View, including Palo Alto, Menlo Park and Stanford University. There is no charge for the paper (although subscriptions are provided for contributors of $5 or more); copies are available free at dozens of locations in stores, street-corner racks and public buildings.

The Grapevine's advertising rates are among the lowest in the area, making this an especially affective place to use part of your advertising budget. Our monthly publication schedule, with features to encourage readers to retain their copy the full month, keeps your ad in people's hands for four or five weeks.

We provide a full range of graphic and photographic services to help you prepare your ad copy, but we also encourage you to submit your own artwork or ads clipped from other publications

We offer a contract discount on all advertising space: if you agree to advertise for four issues or longer, the rates are reduced 10 %, regardless of changes in copy or ad size (layout and photo fees, if any, are excluded). Pre-payment of ads is appreciated, or we will bill you within two weeks of publication.

Advertising Rates

Ad Size	Printed Dimensions		Space Charge	Layout Fee (optional)	
	Width	Height			
Per Column Inch	3 1/4" x	1"	$ 5	$ 1	For Photo Work: Add $2.50 per shot (screen, increase or reduction)
"Business Card"	3 1/4" x	2"	$ 10	$ 2	
Eighth Page	3 1/4" x 4 7/8" 6 3/4" x 2 7/16" 10 1/8" x 1 5/8"		$ 23	$ 4	
Quarter Page	3 1/4" x 9 3/4" 5" x 6 5/8" 6 3/4" x 4 7/8" 10 1/8" x 3 1/4"		$ 45	$ 6	Ad layouts should be submitted
Half Page	5" x 13 1/4" 10 1/8" x 6 5/8"		$ 75	$ 8	5 % oversize (1/16" per inch)
Full Page	10 1/8" x 13 1/4"		$135	$10	

The Grapevine is printed on the Wednesday morning closest to the first day of each month. The deadline for advertising is the Tuesday eight days earlier, usually around the 30th of each month. (We skip one issue during July or August of each year and instead publish one issue about mid-summer.)

In addition to display advertising, we also provide Grapevine 'Little Ads' - classified-type advertising in four categories: 'Declassified', 'Services', 'Self-Help', and 'Personal'. Here, too, our rates are among the lowest: $ 3.50 for 50 words, 10¢ per extra word

For more information, or help in creating your ad, please call CAROL SETTLE or MICHAEL KINDMAN   321-3703

Advertising Rate Sheet

The Advertising Representative

The requirements for a good advertising representative are similar to those of any good sales person. The job calls for a friendly, outgoing individual, with a good measure of persistence, imagination and patience thrown in. A confident manner and good sales pitch are also invaluable when approaching potential customers, as are a copy of the paper and a well drawn up ad rate sheet as illustrated above.

An experienced ad rep is well organized, keeping written records of clients and potential customers and saving him or herself a lot of legwork by telephoning ahead before making a personal call. This helps to eliminate those businesses that are definitely not interested in your services. The telephone pitch doesn't have to be complicated. It may go something like this:

"Hi, I'm Charlotte from the Independent and I wonder if it would be convenient to stop in this afternoon to talk to you about advertising with us."

If a merchant does show interest and the ad rep makes a visit, it's wise to make a pitch early as your time is limited and so is his. Very often you may not even have his or her undivided attention, for if a customer walks in, things will be interrupted and are sure to take a lot longer. Again, the pitch isn't complicated.

"Hi, I'm Charlotte from the <u>Independent</u> and I spoke with you this morning about advertising with us. I've brought a copy of our paper and an ad rate sheet. Why don't you look them over and then tell me what your needs are?"

From here on out be ready to answer questions. Know who reads the paper, what the circulation is and where it's distributed. Be prepared to reveal the average income of your readers and where and on what they are likely to spend money. If there is a nearby business that advertises with success, point this out to the prospective customer. If someone has had fantastic results with a particular ad, quote them without mercy.

Many times merchants will listen to your pitch and want time to think things over. The copy of the paper and a rate sheet will help to make up their minds. Later, when you return, the paper may have already done the selling.

A systematic approach to potential advertisers is a good way to tackle the problem. Make a list of all the shops to hit and people to talk with. Try to gauge just what the chances are for a sell beforehand. If the immediate response is no, leave a couple of copies of the paper and a rate sheet anyway. Later, return to the shop. Even if the folks in the shop don't want to advertise, there is a good chance they may be more than willing to distribute the paper. So ask if you can leave a stack by the door or on a corner of the counter. The disappearing papers may in time convince a shop owner to advertise.

Other Tips For The Advertising Representative

A wise ad rep takes an interest in what the customer is selling and looks for specific items that will market readily. Then he or she knows

how to suggest to the business person the best way to promote the
merchandise in a short, to-the-point format that includes price and
a brief description. The sample ad copy on page 67 illustrates this
point nicely.

A good ad rep also has a feeling for business cycles and seasonal
sales -- swimsuits in summer, snowsuits in winter and shoes in fall
for back to school. Of course, the time to encourage a client to push
these items is during their peak sales period.

Don't neglect smaller ads or hesitate to suggest them on a regular basis, offering a discount of 10 or 15 percent for running them in
five or more consecutive issues. This type of ad can have an additional advantage if the display format's arranged in such a way as to
allow you to insert or change the specific item offered for sale while
maintaining the overall border and format.

While seeking new customers, don't overlook the competing publications. If you see ads that would run well in your paper, don't
hesitate to phone up the merchant and quote a price for the same copy.
And while looking for potential advertising possibilities, consult your
list of those who show promise and mail them a copy of the ad rate
sheet along with your latest issue. Follow this up with a telephone
call.

Then last, but still important, don't forget your faithful and regular
customers. Let them know that you really appreciate their business
by stopping by now and then with helpful suggestions or proposed modifications to their usual copy.

What Makes a Good Display Ad?

The best ads are the ones that are specific and to the point. Good
ad copy should be pleasing in appearance, simple, straightforward.
It should contain a description of the product or service, preferably
a photograph or illustration, the price and any outstanding features
or functions.

Often a merchant will be confused about what to advertise or how

to present ad copy. Help them out by suggesting a specific item. For
example, rather than running a vague add -- Alphonse's Restaurant Has
the Best Natural Food In Town -- why not push Alphonse's Mock Turkey
and Avocado Sandwiches, complete with tempting illustration and a
price of $1.59?

When to Advertise

All businesses have their good seasons and bad ones. Obviously
bicycles and beach blankets don't move very fast during Christmas
time in Maine. But items like radios, jewelry, televisions and books
peak in sales at this time of year.

One way to help shopkeepers decide when to advertise is to get
them to graph the ups and downs of their retail sales. Such a
graph might look like the one illustrated below. The trick is to

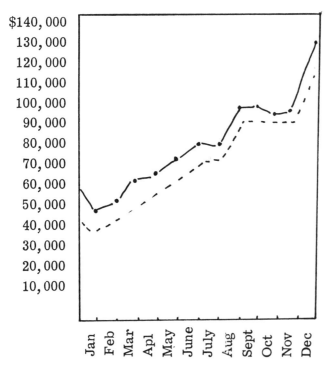

Graph of advertising
expenditures paral-
leling gross sales.

make the advertising budget parallel the graph of gross sales. For example, if sales of cameras are heaviest around Christmas, then a photo supply store would do well to concentrate its advertising expenditures at that time. Similarly, stationery and clothing stores do well to begin back-to-school sales in August. For household items, ads just before payday and at the beginning of the month tend to be better pullers, because people tend to buy things when they have the cash. If you choose to time ads in this manner, be sure to run them with enough lead time rather than too late.

Other Types of Ads

Classified and Want Ads: Three-line classified ads for a flat rate of $2 can bring in revenue, provide a necessary community service and increase your circulation. Rates for businesses should be higher than for individuals. Here too it's best to have the advertiser include the price. If the paper is a weekly, it's worth while to sell multiple insertions at a discount. Descriptive words in these ads often improve the results -- antique oak table, rebuilt pickup, lush, exotic ferns.

Business Cards: Very often a good portion of one page of the paper can be reserved for small, business-card-size ads, often arranged in what's known as a business directory. Most likely these ads can be arranged in categories and run in the same location for extensive lengths of time from a few months to a year.

Legal Notices: Free papers are not eligible to carry legal advertising, but if your paper has paid circulation, then you can run legal notices from local governments, agencies, courts, banks or similar institutions. Check these sources out. If an agency knows that your paper exists, it may use your services. Similar to classified ads, these too are usually charged by the line.

Political Ads: Political ads around election time are great sources of revenue. But beware. All such ads should be paid for in advance and for good reason. Even the winning candidate's war chest is often in the red come election eve.

Stuffers: "Stuffers," or special preprinted advertising inserts stuffed into the center of your paper as a second section, can cause problems. Often trashy in appearance, these inserts have been known to cause a lot more grief than they are worth. This in part is due to the fact that their rates are lower than regular advertising and also because they're preprinted and you have no control over the content or appearance. One sly way to discourage this kind of business is to charge outrageous rates for the privilege of using your paper. Another method of dealing with the problem is for you to redesign a full page ad in your paper using the stuffer copy.

Charging for Ad Copy

Advertising is charged by the column inch, that is, the width of the column in your paper times its height in inches. Therefore, a simple ad that is a column wide and five inches high is charged a rate of five column inches. One measuring two columns in width and five inches high would be charged ten column inches and so forth. The number of column inches is then multiplied by a flat rate charge per column inch, yielding the price charged to the customer. At this point discounts come into play. Many papers offer discounts for running over $100 of advertising (ten or fifteen percent off) or discounts for running the same ad a certain number of times in consecutive issues of the paper.

Advertising Checkoff List

One way to keep track of advertising for each issue of a newspaper is through the use of an ad checkoff list. For any given issue of the paper, the ad rep should prepare a list that indicates the size of each tiser to ensure that the advertisement appeared exactly the way that the client wanted it to.

If a serious mistake does occur in the ad copy, the easiest way to handle the problem is to offer to run an equivalent ad in the next issue at a considerable discount or, in extreme cases, for free. Sometimes, though, it's difficult to make restitution, as in the case of a one-time sale, or when there is a serious misprint in price or location. When this happens, the best policy is to be sympathetic and generous. Being hard-nosed, especially when you have made an honest mistake, will earn you nothing but a bad reputation among the business community.

Of course, there are a few disagreeable customers who may continually complain and gripe about small or imagined imperfections in their ad copy. Know when and where to draw the line with these types and be willing to relinquish their business if they tie up too much of your energy.

Collecting on Overdue Accounts

Another disagreeable part of advertising, which can run you ragged if you let it, has to do with the collection of overdue bills. Unfortunately, because of a common attitude among merchants about the marginal value of advertising, your bill may be the one last paid. For those who have failed to square their accounts after a certain time, often scribbling a handwritten note on the margin of a second statement will provide enough incentive to get them to pay. From handwritten notes, pressure can escalate to friendly telephone calls and to insistent ones and from there to a personal visit. The point here is not to let delinquent accounts drain your energy and enthusiasm for more important matters. Learn to keep close tabs on unpaid accounts; don't extend credit where unwarranted or past a certain point. After a while, you will know who the slow-paying but basically honest merchants are and will be able to separate them from those who have no intention of settling

ad in column width and height, the price paid, any discount given or
charge for blowup or reduction.   This list totaled gives an idea not
only of the total ad revenue for each issue but also the percentage of
space devoted to advertising versus copy.   The list should be available during layout and checked and double-checked against the flats
before they go to the printer.

Ad Billing

Since the bulk of any paid newspaper's revenues comes from advertising, it's important that careful and meticulous records be kept of
advertising accounts.   The best way to do this is to keep a large account
book or loose-leaf ledger with a page for each client.   You can design
your own account forms and print them up or photocopy them, or you can
purchase something adequate from a stationery supply store.   At the
end of the month, when it's time to send out bills, it's this account
book which tells you who owes what.

Probably the quickest way to handle the ad billing process is to
simply sit down with the billable issues of the paper, going through
them page by page and crossing off the ads with a large red crayon as
you draw up a list of the accounts outstanding.   Alphabetized, this list
is then cross-checked against the ad rep's checkoff list for the billable
issues.   Be sure to include here the ads the ad rep may not have solicited himself and take care not to send out an invoice for those already
paid for in advance, marking these accordingly.

When the alphabetized list is completed, a bill should be prepared in
the advertising account book for each client on the list.   This entry
should include the issue or issues the ad occurred in and the column size
and rate charged, as well as any discount given.   If the advertiser has
a previous balance, that too should be included.

When you mail out the bill, be sure to include a neatly clipped copy
of the ad as it actually appeared in the paper.   It's a good idea, in addition, to mail out an entire copy of the paper prior to billing the adver-

at all. Stay away from the latter, as well as from any other suspected bad risks, or, if you find this difficult, insist that they pay cash in advance.

In the end, for the small number of unscrupulous advertisers who steadfastly refuse to pay, your alternatives are few. First, you can take them to small claims court. This is usually an uncomplicated affair, but be forewarned -- winning a judgment and collecting the money can be two different matters entirely. Next, for a stiff cut, you can give the account to a professional collection agency. Finally, you can give up entirely and write the whole thing off.

Paying the Ad Rep

On a fledgling newspaper, probably the only person who is going to get paid at all in the beginning is the advertising representative. Obviously, what ad reps are paid will depend on the amount of advertising revenue they bring in. Therefore, the most common practice is to pay them on a strict or modified commission basis. A strict commission basis means the rep gets fifteen or twenty per-cent of the price of an ad when it's paid for. A modified commission basis may give them a token salary of, say, $125 weekly and a minimum quota to sell, for example, of $600 in ads. When using a quota system, be sure to include an incentive for exceeding the quota, such as giving the ad rep ten percent for anything sold over the minimum.

Worknotes

Filing System: Get yourself a secondhand set of filing cabinets and a dozen or more shoeboxes and establish a filing routine for incoming copy, press releases, classified ads, bills and other incoming mail. Invaluable is a large rubber stamp to mark the date that each item is received. The shoebox system allows you to toss each incoming item in its appropriate nook to be dealt with immediately. Later, at the end of the month, the boxes can be sorted through and unneeded materials discarded while bills, receipts and other item to be kept are transferred to the filing cabinets for more permanent storage and record-keeping.

General Ledger: If you're really serious about making your paper a financial success, then it's time to consider setting up a good book-keeping system designed especially for your needs. It's wise at this point to seek out professional and expert help. Most likely this will mean consulting a good accountant and tax lawyer and hiring a part-time bookkeeper. Your bookkeeper can set up a general ledger to maintain detailed records of the paper's monetary transactions and cash flow. This will include all the money you receive or pay out, the date of the transaction, what it was for and the like. If you are so fortunate as to be able to pay people, your bookkeeper can also handle your payroll and tax records. Over a period of time, it's the general ledger which will show you how well you're doing, whether you're making it financially or operating at a loss.

Other Records: Two other important records include a subscription filing system and a circulation record book. A subscription filing system consists of subscription cards containing the name, address and starting and expiration date, as well as the billing record, for each subscriber. A good subscription file should be accurate and kept up-to-date. This is especially important if you mail your paper using a second-class permit. The reason for this is that the postal authorities may at any time ask to see your subscription records to make certain you're complying with second-class regulations.

A circulation record is simply a book listing your circulation figures for each issue, the total newsstand sales and number of copies left at other drop-offs and local businesses. A quick glance at the circulation record book lets you know over a period of time just where all those newspapers are actually going.

XII
At The Printers

"You want it good, fast, cheap? Then pick two, mister, and call me tomorrow." This is what one printer advised a pushy customer.

If printers have a well-deserved reputation for not being fun to deal with, so have a lot of customers. The source of almost all of these problems can be found easily enough.

Most of them have to do with a lack of understanding by the customer of the printing process itself.

Because offset printing is a photographic process, what you see is what you get. If the lines on your original aren't straight, they won't be straight on the finished product. With all the modern wizardry in the world, the printer can't make the copy any better than the original you came in with. Understand that if you show up with copy typed on your dusty old college portable, pasted half on green paper, half on goldenrod, with something tacked on out of a local newspaper, the resulting product is not likely to please the eye. No camera made will align those crooked e's. Nor will it improve the pitifully fuzzy text of your well-worn cloth ribbon. Don't expect it -- or the printer, either -- to correct your atrocious spelling.

Tips on Dealing With the Printer

Before approaching the printer, have a fair idea of what you want. Know how many copies you expect to produce and on what size and type of paper. Make a quick mock-up of what you intend to do and get in touch with the printer while it's still in the concept stage. Many times a good printer can save you time, money and heartbreak by pointing out what's possible and what's not. But don't expect him to give you a lesson in the graphic arts. Printing, after all, is a business. The time spent talking to you may well be taking him away from another job.

Give your printshop plenty of time. This means <u>days</u>. As the crusty old printer was trying to intimate to the cranky customer, you can have fast, and possibly good, work, but it won't be cheap. Printing is a complicated, time-consuming affair. A lot goes into it. Allow your shop three or four days to do a newsletter. Allow them a couple of days for something less complicated.

Always leave a half inch of whitespace on all edges of your paste-up. This is necessary for the grippers of the press. Leave 3/4 inch or more space for "gutters" for work that is to be folded. Even if you intend to "bleed" a photograph right off the page, remember that it can't be printed this way. It must be trimmed and that will cost you extra. Likewise, oversized, irregular or specially cut paper is going to cost you more. Expect to pay, of course, for any folding, stapling or collating that your job may call for.

Bibliography

<u>A Manual of Style</u>. 12th ed. Chicago: University
    of Chicago Press, 1979.
    The Bible of punctuation, capitalization,
    abbreviations, hyphenation and so forth. Don't
    be without one.

Arnold, Edmund. <u>Modern Newspaper Design</u>.
    New York: Harper and Row, 1969.
    The definitive book on big city newspaper design.
    Look into it.

Berryman, Gregg. <u>Notes on Graphic Design</u>. Los Altos, CA: William
    Kaufmann, Inc., 1979.
    A notebook of essential design information for the uninitiated.

Burke, Clifford. <u>Printing It</u>. New York: Ballantine Books, 1972.
    If you buy no other book, get this one. It's an excellent guide to graphic
    techniques for the impecunious, all done on an IBM Executive typewriter.

Fenner, Peter and Armstrong, Martha C. <u>Research: A Practical Guide</u>
    <u>to Finding Information</u>. Los Altos, CA: William Kaufmann, Inc., 1981.
    This is a practical guide to finding information for those who find
    libraries forbidding places.

Follett, Wilson. <u>Modern American Usage</u>. New York: Hill & Wang, 1966.
    A good reference book for correct usage.

Garst, Robert and Bernstein, Theodore. <u>Headlines and Deadlines: A</u>
    <u>Manual for Copy Editors</u>. New York: Columbia University Press, 1961.
    Good advice on headline composition and copy editing from two editors
    of the <u>New York Times</u>.

Gill, Eric. <u>Essay on Typography</u>. London: J. M. Dent & Sons, 1960.
    Everything you ever wanted to know about typography.

Halftone Methods for the Graphic Arts. Manual Q-3, expanded ed.
    Rochester, NY: Eastman Kodak, 1972.
    This manual, along with Kodak manual Q-1 on basic photography, will
    give you a thorough understanding of the halftone process.

Hanks, Kurt; Belliston, Larry; and Edwards, Dave. Design Yourself!
    Los Altos, CA: William Kaufmann, Inc., 1980.
    This book is loaded with dozens of thinking and visualizing exercises
    to help you analyze, plan and communicate.

_____. 1980. Draw! A Visual Approach to Learning, Thinking and
    Communicating. Los Altos, CA: William Kaufmann, Inc.
    Almost a thousand drawings, cartoons, sketches and photographs to
    aid you in understanding the techniques of drawing and graphic design.

Hill, Mary and Cochran, Wendell. Into Print. Los Altos, CA: William
    Kaufmann, Inc., 1977.
    Great practical handbook on writing, illustrating and publishing.

Hough, Henry Beetle. Country Editor. Riverside, CT: Chatham Press,
    1974.
    Originally published in 1940, this is a classic on small-town journalism
    and editing.

How to Do Leaflets, Newsletters, and Newspapers. Somerville, MA:
    New England Free Press, 1976.
    This is an excellent little manual -- of activist origins -- crammed
    full of useful information.

How to Produce a Small Newspaper. Harvard, MA: Harvard Common
    Press, 1978.
    Produced by the editors of the Harvard Post, this excellent book gives
    details of a newspaper as a small business.

Kennedy, Bruce M. Community Journalism: A Way of Life. Ames, IA:
    Iowa State University Press, 1974.
    The ins and outs of a country press.

Lee, Marshall. Bookmaking. New York: R. R. Bowker, 1965.
    More information on bookmaking than you'll ever need.

McKinney, John. How to Start Your Own Community Newspaper. Port
    Jefferson, NY: Meadow Press, 1977.
    Worth reading, but overpriced and underorganized.

One Book/Five Ways. Los Altos, CA: William Kaufmann, Inc., 1977.
    This is an experiment in which a single manuscript was submitted to
    five different university presses to see how they handled the production,
    design, editing and sales of a prospective book. Very illuminating for
    those struggling with manuscripts and publishers.

Strunk, William Jr. and White, E. B. The Elements of Style. 2d ed.
    New York: Macmillan, Inc., 1972.
    The classic "little book" that is absolutely essential for writers and
    editors. Explains all those things your high school English teacher
    could never pound into your head.

Watkins, Don. Guide to Newspaper Design and Layout. Columbia, SC:
    Columbia Newspapers, 1976.
    The do's and don'ts of ad layout. Give this to your ad representative.

Willis, F. H. Fundamentals of Layout. New York: Dover Publications
    Inc., 1971.
    This book is designed for magazine layout more than newspapers.
    Worth reading.

Other Useful References

The New American Roget's Thesaurus in Dictionary Form. Philip D.
  Morehead, prep. by. New York: Signet Classics, 1978.
  This edition is available in paperback. Very helpful in finding the
  right word.

Webster's New World 33,000 Word Book. Shirley M. Miller, comp.
  by. The World Publishing Co., 1977.
  A must for poor spellers. This little blue hardback, based on the
  Webster's New World Dictionary, gives you the correct spelling
  without the clutter of definition.

Webster's New Collegiate Dictionary. Springfield, MA: G. & C.
  Merriam Company, 1980.
  This dictionary is big enough to be useful but not so large that
  you'll be tripping over it.

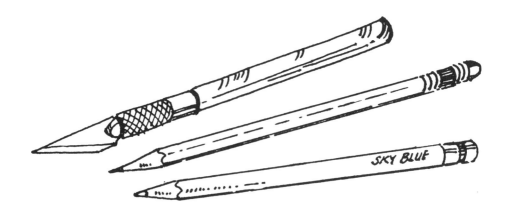

INDEX

Designed by Jan Sutter.
Front matter and page composition by Spectra Media.
Composition by Frank's Type.
Printed by Malloy Lithographing, Inc.
on sixty pound Glatfelter
in an edition of 5,000 paperbound copies.